Memoirs

of

Mercy

by

Dionna K. Trice

Bloomington, IN Milton Keynes, UK

authorHOUSE

AuthorHouse™
1663 Liberty Drive, Suite 200
Bloomington, IN 47403
www.authorhouse.com
Phone: 1-800-839-8640

AuthorHouse™ UK Ltd.
500 Avebury Boulevard
Central Milton Keynes, MK9 2BE
www.authorhouse.co.uk
Phone: 08001974150

First published by AuthorHouse 6/22/2006

ISBN: 1-4259-3867-1 (sc)

Printed in the United States of America
Bloomington, Indiana

This book is printed on acid-free paper.

All scriptures have been quoted from the authorized
King James Version of the Bible.

The accounts in **Memoirs of Mercy** are real. However, some of the names have been changed as an act of "mercy."

DEDICATION

Memoirs of Mercy *is dedicated to my husband, Pastor Frederick Lamont Trice, my best friend and confidant. Thanks for walking with me through the corridors of these Memoirs of Mercy. Thank you for reminiscing in each of the alcoves that branched from the halls. Thank you for your daily prayers. Thank you for your unwavering commitment. Thank you for your boundless encouragement. Thank you for your selflessness. Thank you for the best ten years of my life.*

I love you.

Your "Pooh,"

Dionna

THANK YOU

A very special thank you to my Lord and Savior Jesus Christ *for giving me a whole new set of memoirs—and bringing me through the old ones.*

To Minister Pauletta "Mother" Fields. *Thanks for just being there. Words could not express my level of gratitude to God for sending me you. I met you on my birthday, and you have been a precious gift ever since. I thank God for you, and pray that Fields of Gold greeting cards expand from sales around the country, into sales around the world.*

A special "Thank You" to the One Accord International Worship Center (OAIWC) family. *Thanks for your sincerity and faithfulness. The Lord has truly smiled upon me and Pastor Trice to have brought us into relationship with such good-hearted people like you. God bless each of you!*

To Pastors Mike & Tammy Dixon. *"Our family." Good friends with good hearts. We love you and can't wait to see how the Lord blesses you for your faithfulness. Tammy, thanks for the last-minute editing. Mike, thanks* for the awesome book cover design. We look forward to visiting you at **www. Gods 12ᵗʰ Man. org.**

I would also like to thank each person mentioned within these memoirs. If it weren't for you, I would not have found my destination "in the place of God."

A special thanks to each of you, my family and friends, who have supported this work. God Bless!

Love,
Dionna K. Trice

FOREWORD
by Pastor Frederick Trice

What do you do when you have been the victim of someone else's power, control, and influence over your life? Where do you go when the only source of love and trust has betrayed and rejected you? Who can you trust to tell about the abandonment, abuse, anger, bitterness, frustration, molestation, neglect, and deep-deep rooted sorrow that floods your soul?

There are a number of Christians suffering the affects of a devious and shameful illness. They are the people who have been victimized by mothers, fathers, clergy, friends, relatives, and other individuals in positions of authority. It is unfathomable for a Christian to say "I have been abandoned, abused, molested, raped, rejected, neglected, and spiritually, I am dying."

Within the walls of the human heart there is a desperate cry for help. However, it has been muffled by the "don't ask, don't tell" policies enacted by religious leaders who forbid you to be what God has made you—human. We are all, to some degree or another, victims of a stronghold. We have built fortresses made of grains of guilt, sands of shame, and stones of fear.

Co-Pastor Dionna Trice, in her tell-all book entitled **Memoirs of Mercy**, offers a balm and cure for the infectious and devious pandemic called *silence.* Her willingness to break the code of silence and come clean will empower many. Like Christ, she dared to stand trial on the pavement of the public court for a crime she did not commit. Her willingness to allow her accusers to levy charges against her demonstrates that her only motivation is love. While many self-righteous religious leaders may criticize these writings, "it is Christ that died, yea rather, that is risen again." Romans 8: 34 (KJV)

I was blessed to witness and experience a true miracle. I saw my wife literally transform before my very eyes. I saw her crawl like a caterpillar. I saw a poor fragile creature being tossed to and fro with the winds of adversity; swayed by the seas of others' expectations; and nearly trodden on the paths of life's trail.

I watched the caterpillar endure the threats of life's storms. I saw this caterpillar turn the silk fabric of God's Word into a protective cocoon. One day, I noticed a miracle had transpired. The hopeless creature which sheltered itself from the threatening elements of life was transfigured. It no longer crawled but took flight. It emerged from the earth bound species it once was into a beautiful transformed spirit. With her wings spread wide and a coat of many colors, she ascended into freedom. The transformed creature began exploring the world from a different view. She was heaven bound with no limitations. She flew by the light of the Son, and the various spectrums of color which were once hidden were now revealed. What happened in that cocoon? A powerful discovery was made, a miracle was experienced, and a transformation took place. This is the fruit of the journey I witnessed in my wife Dionna Trice. And now, she has made it possible for others to experience what she discovered in her cocoon—the Memoirs of Mercy.

CONTENTS

INTRODUCTION

Why me? Why didn't my father want me? Why did I find myself looking for love in all the wrong places? Why did I go through abandonment, rejection, loss, death (of family/friends), betrayal, isolation, conflict, disease, hurt, and personal near-death experiences? Why was I still in existence, like a flag that had been tattered through the rigorous tactics of war—yet raised in final victory? Why was I the one who always stood out like a sore thumb? Why did I have to work so hard, while blessings came so easily to others? Was I cursed? Was I paying for the sins of my fathers? Did I do something wrong? God, do you hate me? Why not just let me die?

These were the questions that plagued my weary mind, and entrapped my bitter soul. After much laborious meditation, reflection, and illumination by the Holy Spirit, I came to the realization that the purpose of **Abandonment**—was so that God could preserve me. **Rejection**—to show that I could be restored. **Loss**—so that He could find me. **Death**—so that He could convey His resurrection power, and comfort me. **Betrayal**—so that He could show me His faithfulness. **Isolation**—to affirm that He would always be there. **Conflict**—to prove that He would fight all of my battles. **Disease & Hurt**—so that I would know Him as Healer. He wanted me to stop placing human imperfections upon Him. He didn't abandon me. He's not the one who rejected me. He would never betray me.

Now I know that a happily ever after is possible. A change for the better is possible. Healing is possible. Finding true love is possible. Someone can love you despite internal & external imperfections. It is possible to release all of your emotional baggage. It is possible to trust again—to believe again. It is possible to live—and you haven't lived until you've had a relationship with God. It is possible to put on spiritual lenses and see clearly. It is possible to walk into destiny and have purpose in your life.

This book is a collection of memoirs—the sum total of which reflect God's mercy (His compassion) in my life. He said that He would never leave nor forsake us, and that He would be with us always, even until the ends of the earth.

Hebrew 13:5
…for he hath said, I will never leave thee, nor forsake thee.

Matthew 28:20
…and, lo, I am with you alway[s], even unto the end of the world. Amen.

Memoirs of Mercy is a survival guide addressed to anyone who has been fatherless, or suffered devastation through loss, rejection, isolation and abandonment. It shows you how to keep the faith—even after you've done all the right things, yet all hell is breaking loose around you. It is to the person who feels trapped in their life's circumstances as a result of generational curses. This book is for the person who has tried everything, but still needs supernatural deliverance.

God has restored my life after enduring prolonged seasons of emotional pain. I want to share these memoirs with you, and pray that your healing be expedited through the life that He has given me. Be blessed and encouraged after reading the following passages. Let this book challenge you to identify the root causes of negative cycles in your life. Let it inspire you to prioritize what's really important.

It's OK. It's going to be OK. Now my friend, let's walk together, hand in hand, through the corridors of the **Memoirs of Mercy.**

I WITNESS

When I was a little girl, my mother and I attended a local Baptist church in St. Louis City. Papa (my step-grandfather) was the Associate Pastor; Granny (my grandmother) taught Sunday School, and was President of the Baptist Berean District. My mother taught children's music for the Sunbeam Choir, and did administrative work in the church. Most Sundays, we were required to arrive extra early in the morning. The deacon board consisted of elderly men who would cook breakfast on Sunday mornings for the ministry staff—and I would stand nearby and watch as they poured milk into the eggs and scrambled them in a big black cast iron skillet. The aroma of fluffy eggs, bacon, coffee and toast would fill the entire lower level of our huge, gothic, gray-stoned church. They would prepare a special bacon-egg-toast sandwich just for me. I remember sitting on a tall stool eating breakfast at the kitchen counter, while grape jelly oozed down my sandwich, my face, and my dress. I felt so important.

The deacons would lead Sunday morning devotion, singing Dr. Watts Negro spirituals, such as "I Love The Lord, He Heard My Cry,"—and the moaning would echo for blocks. I always sat next to my Granny, asking her to interpret the drawn-out, moaning lyrics so that I could sing along. After singing, she would show me how to pay tithes in church. I didn't really understand tithing (paying ten percent of your income to the Lord) at the time, but I always followed her instructions and put my twenty cents in the envelope. The church's First Lady was a true saint by every definition of the word, but the Pastor, Reverend Doctor, was a whoremonger. He was portly, fair-skinned with wavy black hair and grey eyes. Most Sundays, he would preach, "Don't do as I do. Do as I say do." Reverend Doctor would preach a riveting message, and seemingly in one conclusive motion, he would give a loud shout, throw his handkerchief in the air, spin around while his robe parachuted, and catch it before hitting the ground. By then, every member, fully charged with emotionalism, was jumping out of their seats shouting "Hallelujah!"

Under Reverend Doctor's leadership, it was OK to smoke and drink excessively, hang out in taverns, and "get your creep on." But most members knew better. They knew that there was a better way of life—one of striving for purity in God—and lived accordingly.

My curiosity would get the best of me. I'd skip around the church, and hide in little cubby holes. Times were different. People were different. I could stray from the adults, and no one feared that I'd been abducted. I always felt safe at church. One day, while skipping through the lower level, I stumbled upon Reverend kissing the church pianist (who, by the way, was not his wife). His tongue was so far down her throat, he could have given her a tonsillectomy. Another time, I found him in a compromising position with yet another woman in an inconspicuous dark room underneath the stairs. Reverend Doctor made his rounds throughout the church—and because I frequently caught him in the act, he would intimidate me by saying degrading things to hurt my feelings. He always found himself between a rock and a hard place with me, because my grandparents were his best friends.

I used to hear intimate conversations between Reverend Doctor and his main mistress on the side porch of the church. I was only about five or six years old, but these are the things I witnessed with my own eyes and ears. As a teenager, I observed him getting arrested on the news for charges of a sexual nature—but the members always swept his lifestyle under the rug. To this day, many women still reveal to me the vulgar things that Reverend Doctor said to them—one is even a relative.

One day, a rumor spread throughout the church that a certain member was having an affair with a married man. This member fit the description of Mamma—but it was NOT my mother. Eventually, the true identity of the mistress was revealed, but the damage had already been done. Much of the congregation had falsely accused Mamma and treated her with such cruelty that she resigned her membership.

THE DAY OF PENTECOST

Mamma and I ultimately joined another church. It was a local Pentecostal church in North St. Louis City. Pentecostals believe in being filled with the Holy Ghost and speaking in tongues, which was new to us.

Acts 2:1-4

And when the day of Pentecost was fully come, they were all with one accord in one place. And suddenly there came a sound from heaven as of a rushing mighty wind, and it filled all the house where they were sitting. And there appeared unto them cloven tongues like as of fire, and it sat upon each of them. And they were all filled with the Holy Ghost, and began to speak with other tongues, as the Spirit gave them utterance.

Over the years, Mamma began singing with a traveling gospel choir. She also sang in the church Adult Choir and was an integral part of the Prison Ministry, Funeral Committee, Church Bulletin Committee, and Media Ministry. Most weekdays, she came straight from work to design a six-to-eight page church bulletin for our congregation of over three thousand members. Every fourth Sunday, she accompanied the Prison Ministry Team to minister to convicted felons. Children were not allowed to participate in prison outreach, therefore

I, Mamma's only child, would have dinner with various families from the church and they would bring me back for Sunday evening service. Mamma would pick me up after service when she came back from prison outreach.

By the age of ten, I knew that I wanted to sing. So, soon after my eleventh birthday, I joined the youth choir and continued until I left for college at the age of seventeen. I loved church. I loved the feeling of family. I loved the smiling faces. I loved the familiarity and stability. I loved the big, beautiful edifice.

I had a few friends. Most people in the church were genuinely nice, good, people. But there were a number of affluent inner circles within the church that I could never become a part of. I was never good enough. I was poor, chubby, and being raised by a single parent. Early advancement in public schools placed me in grades with older students, so I was always the youngest in academic classes as well as Sunday School. I was too young to befriend the older children, and too old to befriend the younger.

The one thing I hated about church was being there almost every day—sometimes until midnight—while my mother and others from the Bulletin Committee designed, collated, and stapled over three-thousand church bulletins. There were a number of occasions when Mamma was the only worker left. During those times, I was alone with her, manually collating and stapling the bulletins. Once that work was complete, she could be found in the Media Room, duplicating tapes and preparing them for sale after church service.

Some workers were paid, but my mother worked diligently for eight years with no pay. The First Lady of the church even told Mamma, for no apparent reason, that she didn't like her. But Mamma never quit. The various Church Bulletin workers would come and go, but my mother was a constant. At that time, I didn't understand why she persevered. I didn't understand that God was causing roots to sprout underneath me—positioning me like a tree planted by the rivers of water, weathering the storms of life.

Psalm 1:1-3

Blessed is the man that walketh not in the counsel of the ungodly, nor standeth in the way of sinners, nor sitteth in the seat of the scornful. But his delight is in the law of the LORD; and in his law doth he meditate day and night. **And he shall be like a tree planted by the rivers of water**, that bringeth forth his fruit in his season; his leaf also shall not wither; and whatsoever he doeth shall prosper.

He wanted to show me that He is a rewarder of those that diligently seek Him. God rewards faithfulness. He was showing me that you don't run A-WAY because things don't go YOUR-WAY.

Hebrews 11:6

But without faith it is impossible to please him: for he that cometh to God must believe that he is, and that he is a **rewarder** of them that diligently seek him.

Mamma's involvement with the Funeral Committee allowed me to accompany her into the homes of deceased persons' families to plan funeral arrangements and write obituaries. She would lead the family in prayer, and we would proceed by discussing the deceased's life, and the order in which the family wanted the obituary written. There were times when the family would argue over arrangements, and Mamma was the voice of reason.

The Pentecostal Church we attended was very strict. Therefore, I was forbidden to wear pants, go to parties, movies, or wear makeup. The color red was a symbol of Jezebel. And braiding hair was sinful. One summer, the church youth choir wanted to spend the day at Six Flags Amusement Park. The question was raised, in the church, whether amusement parks were sinful. After much debate, the elders conceded that they were not. So we all went to Six Flags, but the girls had to wear skirts and dresses.

We were taught in church that once you were born again and thereafter committed a sin, you had to get re-born again or re-saved. If we escaped Hell, that was good enough. A common phrase was, "I'm doin' my best to make it in!" Every Sunday, the altar was filled with so many regular church members that there was little room for new converts. During my teen years, it occurred that something was wrong with me. I had been re-saved about seventy-five times! At church, they would show us movies about the End Times, the Rapture (the advent when Christ comes back to take His Church [the Christians] to Heaven), and the Great Tribulation (persecution of the Christian church). My fear was if the Rapture came, I would be left behind because I kept sinning. I was even afraid to read the Book of Revelations.

When I was about sixteen years old, Mamma and I were living in a duplex upstairs from my great-grandmother, Big Mamma. One evening, I went downstairs to talk with Big Mamma and her front door was wide-open. All of her lights were on. Her back door was open. Big Mamma was nowhere to be found! My first thought was that the Rapture had come and I was left behind on earth with all of the remaining heathens (the non-believers in Jesus Christ). As I was thinking about how I could collect food, hide out to avoid Christian persecution, and not take the Mark of the Beast, Big Mamma came inside from the backyard and said she had been talking with our next-door neighbors. What a relief!

The frustration began to mount. There was little balanced living. It seemed good Christian living consisted of more *don'ts* than *do's*. Since I couldn't seem to stay saved, I decided to backslide (intentionally and willfully sin against God) once and for all. So, when I was seventeen I went away to college at Southeast Missouri State University (SEMO) and rebelled. The first things I purchased upon arrival were a pair of jeans, and a jogging suit. I cut my hair in the style of the then-popular rap group, "Salt N Peppa," bought red lipstick, and asked the sorority girls to teach me the latest dances. I eventually joined a sorority and attended the Greek college parties from Thursday through Saturday every week. My grades reflected such overindulgence.

I joined the SEMO St. James Choir. The founder of the choir, Stan, eventually asked me to become the official Choir Director, but I was forced to decline. It was an awesome honor to be thought of so highly by my peers, but after becoming a new Resident Advisor I was unable to travel with them due to the flexible scheduling of my new job.

I still loved singing. The choir gave me this connection, like a life-saving transfusion. I could feel God when I sang songs *about* Him and *to* Him. Although I considered myself an official backslider and no longer went to church, I had a desire to be in His presence. My relationship was becoming personal. Even though I'd walked away from

God, He'd never walked away from me. Years later, the Holy Spirit brought me to this realization:

You *are* your father's child! There is nothing you can do to change that! In **John 3:1-7**, there was a religious leader named Nicodemus, who asked Jesus the following question:

> ..."How can a man be born when he is old? Can he enter the second time into his mother's womb, and be born?" Jesus answered, "Verily, verily, I say unto thee, Except a man be born of Water and of the Spirit, he cannot enter into the kingdom of God. That which is born of the flesh is flesh; and that which is born of the Spirit is spirit. Marvel not that I said unto thee, ye must be born again."

Once you are born of your natural father, there is absolutely nothing you can do to change that. You could spit on your father, curse at him, hit him, run him over with a car, bite him, or strangle him, but he is still your father. It's the story of the prodigal son in **Luke 15:11-32**. He lived a riotous life and brought himself so low that he was eating the same husks that he was supposed to be feeding the pigs. But one day, he came to his senses. He repented and his father accepted him back. He prematurely squandered his entire inheritance and brought himself into a low estate—but he was still his father's son!

It's that way in the spirit. Once you become born again or saved (accept Jesus Christ as your Lord and Savior), there is nothing you can do to become un-born. The Bible says that there is only one unforgivable sin—the sin of blasphemy against the Holy Ghost:

<u>Matthew 12:31</u>

Wherefore I say unto you, All manner of sin and blasphemy shall be forgiven unto men: but the blasphemy against the Holy Ghost shall not be forgiven unto men.

The Holy Spirit began to show me the bigger picture by asking the following questions:

Which man in the Bible did not have weaknesses?

Which man, besides Jesus, in the Bible was without sin?

Which man in the Bible had absolutely no insecurities?

To date, I have yet to find one man. This means that you and I fit within the category of actually being "human." We all have desires and passions; and they are not always righteous. But as we grow in God, and Walk in His Spirit, then we will not fulfill the lusts of our flesh. **(Galatians 5:16)**

Once we accept Christ as our Savior, we are His children. Yes, we mess up. We may do things to hurt our Lord (as He is a God of emotions), but we repent for those mistakes and move forward. What does it mean to repent? It means to spiritually turn one-hundred-eighty degrees from our disobedient ways, and follow in the ways of Christ. To acknowledge that we are sinners and that when His blood was shed on Calvary's cross, He paid the sin debt for us. To acknowledge that Jesus Christ, the True and Living God, is the only One who can wash us clean—inside and out. He can even change our nature. He can deliver from all addictions, sexual perversions, and diseases. He is God—with no outside help or supplements. He is God by reason of His own existence. Twelve-step programs cannot deliver you, but **one** step toward Jesus Christ can change your entire life.

2 Chronicles 7:14

If my people, which are called by my name, shall humble themselves, and pray, and seek my face, and turn from their wicked ways; then will I hear from heaven, and will forgive their sin, and will heal their land.

If we develop a posture of unrepentance, we will lose the favor, inheritance, and rewards that God promises to us on earth, and in eternity. Your actions will have consequences. The same God of mercy is also a God of Judgment. But after you have been born again (saved)

God's spiritual laws forbid you from becoming UN-BORN.

What a relief to finally realize that one mistake or indiscretion would not send me straight to hell! I began to feel free in my spirit. Free to grow. Free to develop a deeper relationship with Christ. Free to move beyond the "birthing" process into spiritual growth and maturity. Free to experience God's mercies, which are new every morning.

Lamentations 3:21-26

This I recall to my mind, therefore have I hope. It is of the LORD'S mercies that we are not consumed, because his compassions fail not. **They are new every morning: great is thy faithfulness**. The LORD is my portion, saith my soul; therefore will I hope in him. The LORD is good unto them that wait for him, to the soul that seeketh him. It is good that a man should both hope and quietly wait for the salvation of the LORD.

As much as I loved the Lord and the relationship we were developing there were issues between us. Because of my past, I was always on guard for someone to leave me, break promises, break my heart or make me feel unworthy of the best, and I brought it into my relationship with God. In **Hebrews 13:5,** the Lord said that he will never leave you nor forsake you. I couldn't relate to that. The 23rd Psalm? Get real! What man could possibly have that much compassion? All this poetic talk about cups running over, leading me beside still waters, and restoring my soul? Come On! Oh, and read this one:

Psalm 91:4

He shall cover thee with his feathers, and under his wings shalt thou trust: his truth shall be thy shield and buckler.

Let's not even talk about trust. I had no consistent male covering, so I could not fully comprehend the thought of staying under God's wings (within His protective borders)—nor could I comprehend His love for me.

My Natural Fathers

Daddy

My friends who grew up around abusive, alcoholic fathers, gravitated towards abusive, alcoholic boyfriends. Most of my fatherless friends had babies out of wedlock. A couple of friends, whose fathers gave up their call to ministry, became lesbians. Another friend who was born out of an extra-marital affair became bitter and finds comfort in smothering her young child because her father denies her existence to his "legitimate" family. As a young adult, I gravitated toward relationships with young men who, like my father, were a lot of fun to be around, but they always stood me up, let me down, or broke my heart.

You could hear my father, Thomas, laughing a mile away. He always told stories—and to "beef-up" the story a little, he would begin to embellish. He knew that he was lying, and so did anyone listening—but he just had a way of telling a story.

He was six feet tall, fair-skinned, well groomed, weighed over four-hundred pounds, and women of all persuasions loved him. Daddy was a very handsome, jovial, outgoing person. He was liked by most, never met a stranger and loved Oldies but Goodies. One time, while listening to the radio, the DJ played one of Daddy's favorites, "Beauty's Only Skin Deep." He started wiggling to the beat of the music, smiling, singing, snapping his fingers, raising his eyebrows, and closing his eyes. Then, he would say, "Girl, you don't know nuthin' 'bout this!" And for the next couple of hours that followed, he'd periodically burst out with one-liners singing, "Beauty's Only Skin Deep—Yeah! Yeah! Yeah!"

Daddy had a missing leg from a previous accident. He was a United States Vietnam War Veteran, who faithfully served his country having obtained a Purple Heart, along with an Oak Leaf Cluster. Daddy had a very creative, artistic way about him. Unfortunately, poor choices led him down a path of destruction.

Upon his return from the war in the late 1960's, there were no special jobs—or special treatment for the veterans. He (like hundreds of thousands of Vietnam veterans) was subject to the brutal return to American society—facing discrimination, alcoholism, drug abuse, unemployment, and run-in's with the law. It has even been common knowledge (the numbers vary from study-to-study) that three times more Veterans committed suicide after the war—than died during the war as a result of Post Traumatic Stress Disorder (or some called it "Shell-Shocked"). And even more vets joined the increasing homeless population—finding it difficult to maintain gainful employment and family relationships.

Daddy, just as a myriad of his comrades, fell into this vicious trap. Mamma said that when they were first married in 1969, Daddy dropped to the ground after hearing the sounds of children playing with firecrackers. He had a flashback—thinking he was seeking cover from enemy fire in a Vietnam war-zone.

In the 1970's, with diminished hope for gainful employment, Daddy became a gangster. They called him "Big Tom," or "Machine Gun Tom." He drove a big luxury car he had custom painted so when the sun hit it you could see flicks of sparkles in the paint. Daddy wore custom-made suits, big hats, owned drug houses, carried machine guns, and surrounded himself with countless women. Thus, my parents' marriage did not survive. Mamma maintained legal custody of me, and over the years, my communication with Daddy was minimal. Whenever we did speak with each other, he always made promises which he would break—this used to break my heart.

When I was around twelve, I had the opportunity to spend the summer with him. I was elated to be with my Daddy, his wife, and my siblings. That year, I would find out that I also had an eighteen-year-old brother that my father "forgot" to mention, along with a Vietnamese sister whom I've never met.

The time I spent with my father that summer was filled with activity. These were no lazy days—we were quite entrepreneurial. Daddy had a big neighborhood barbecue sale a couple of times a month. My step-mother had neighborhood fish-fry sales. And my step-brother and I made shaved-ice slushes that summer.

Daddy also sold drugs out of his house. Not knowing any different, I thought he was just popular and had a lot of friends. I had no idea of the dangers I was exposed to everyday. There were no boundaries set for me at his house. It didn't matter to Daddy where I went as long as I notified him of my destination. During that time, a relative of my stepmother would come by the house frequently. He was a young man with a charming and easygoing personality. My father loved him. He did housework and was polite. But when no one else was home, he would have repeated unprotected sex with me. Many years later, this same man was convicted of and incarcerated for rape charges against another woman. My father never knew, and I have never revealed this until now.

Before the first month of that summer ended, my mother prematurely came to take me away. She said that the Lord told her to come and get me—not allowing me to pack any belongings. I grabbed what could immediately fit into my hands, and we swiftly vacated the premises as if escaping from Alcatraz. Within days, Daddy's house was raided by the police. At that time, I resented Mamma for taking me away from my Daddy. I thought that she just didn't want me to be happy. Sometimes I thought she was mean, and hated me because I looked just like him. In this instance, she was obeying God and saving my life!

My relationship with Daddy didn't improve. He failed to show up for my high school graduation. I remember crying while sitting in the back seat of my mother's grey Ford Tempo that night. Then, piercing through my puffy, crying eyes appeared a burgundy limousine. It was my friend, Dwayne, from church. He had previously asked my mother if he could take me out for graduation. She agreed as long as I was home by midnight. He escorted me from my mother's car to the limousine across the street. Upon entry, yellow roses were scattered all over the plush velvet back seat. We had lobsters and daiquiris (virgin of course) for dinner, and lots of laughs. Dwayne's kindness that night sutured my wounded heart.

Daddy avoided my phone calls for a while. When I did finally make contact with him over the phone, I cursed him out. I told him that he wasn't my father. I said, "A person only graduates from high school once, and you didn't even care enough to show up. Then, you didn't have a real reason for not coming. F*** you! I hate you! You're not my father! You're not even a real man! I hardly ever ask you for anything! And when I do—you don't give me anything!"

He responded with, "Baby, you're right—you're just speaking your mind—and you're right."

From that point, until the age of about twenty-one years old, my relationship with Daddy grew even more strained. I was as the man in the Bible who sat at the pool of Bethesda for thirty-eight years (John 5:1-10)— "I had no man" to help me. I had no man to love me enough—to care enough to heal me.

Over the years Daddy's lucrative criminal lifestyle was the impetus that led to constant harassment by the police (and rightfully so). During one period of incarceration, vagrants broke into Daddy's house in the attempt to seek shelter. While trying to keep warm, they turned the furnace to extremely high levels. As a result, Daddy's house burned down, and he lost everything.

There was a time after I recommitted my life to the Lord that Daddy got saved, and started living right. This time was short-lived, but I'm glad that it's a permanent part of my memories:

> Daddy had been hit by a truck. His back and leg were broken in several places. He was in a coma

on a ventilator, and the doctors didn't think he would make it through the night. At that time, my husband Frederick and I were only friends. My mother asked if he would go to the hospital to pray for Daddy. Frederick ministered to my father while in a coma. Tears began streaming down Daddy's cheeks. Within four days, he went from dying in a coma, to getting out of his bed to look out of the window. For months thereafter, my father had completely stopped abusing alcohol and drugs and tried to make up for the time we'd lost.

I occasionally spent the night at Daddy's home. We would laugh and talk throughout the night and of course, he'd tell lots of stories. Laughing until we cried, I'm sure the neighbors thought we were drunk. When I awakened in the mornings, he'd prepare special breakfasts for me. He would also take my unmentionables, and warm them in the oven so that when I got dressed, they would feel "toasty" as they clung to my body. I never knew Daddy could be so sensitive, and so warm. I never knew that he could make me feel so special.

One day I called Daddy to tell him I was coming by to visit. He told me not to come over. He said, "I'm doing something I'm not supposed to do." On Memorial Day in 1998, Daddy was having a "drug and alcohol" party with friends. Apparently, he began to asphyxiate. His "friends" became afraid, cleaned up all of their paraphernalia, and ran up the street to a pay phone to call for an ambulance.

Needless to say, Daddy was dead-on-arrival. His "friends" left him there. Yes! This *is* something to remember! He lived a life surrounded by drugs and alcohol, and died as he'd lived.

Daddy just couldn't seem to let go of his old friends. They eventually cost him his life. They didn't really love him. They could have called for an ambulance from his house. What Daddy didn't realize was God would have given him new friends. He would've met lots of new brothers and sisters at church, and at other wholesome, Christian gatherings—but he chose not to attend such functions.

My friend, our life is surrounded by the choices we make. This includes the company we keep. I'm not saying that you need to drop your old friends like a hot potato, but begin keeping company with those persons from whom you can learn—those who will expand your current scope of wisdom and expectations. You know what they say, "A mind, once stretched, can never return to its original shape!" Surprisingly, you'll find that as you move in a more positive direction, many of your old "friends" will no longer be able to relate to you—and for a moment, you may feel alone. But be encouraged, my friend, you are never alone. God is always there. And I'm praying for you too.

PAPA

The only real father that I knew was my Papa. He stood over six feet tall, thinly built, dark, and well-groomed with mingled grey hair. He always looked fresh. He had a closet full of tailored suits, well polished shoes, and always drove the latest model Cadillac. He had a base-sounding voice, and smelled of expensive cologne. He was a supervisor for the local electric company, which was considered a good job. He and Granny lived in a bungalow in a quiet suburb in University City, Missouri.

When I was a little girl, I would go into the bathroom with Papa in the mornings to watch him shave. He would apply shaving cream on his face and mine. Then he would shave while I, with a blade-less razor, would mimic his every move. I loved my Papa so much that when I took bubble baths, I would pretend that the bubbles were shaving cream and smooth them all over my face the same way he did.

On Saturday afternoons until well into the evening, Papa would go into his study to prepare his sermon for the next morning. He was a minister, and eventually became the pastor of a small Baptist church in Kirkwood, Missouri. I was instructed to never bother him while he studied. But whenever I broke the rules, and whispered his name, he never turned me away.

Papa and I had a special connection. He had an uncanny way of conveying certain academic principles to me in a matter of minutes—whereas it took Mama and my schoolteachers days, and sometimes weeks to teach me the same concepts. He taught me how to tell time in about five minutes and how to count in German in about ten minutes.

At the dinner table, I sat on his right side. Papa would teach me dining etiquette and give a stern look if I accidentally placed my elbows on the table. He never had to spank me. All Papa had to do was give "the look" and shake his finger from side to side, never speaking a word. It was worse than the most horrific punishment— to know that the King was displeased with his Princess.

Papa used to dance with me. I would stand on his feet, and he would take the lead. But I was never just on top of his feet—I was on top of the world. Each pirouette evoked the warmth of Papa's love. He would spin me around—orbiting the white couch in the living room. I was the Princess, dancing with the King. I felt safe—like nothing could hurt me as long as I was in his presence.

Papa and I shared a secret. Mamma forbad me to watch television shows like "Hee Haw" and the "Gong Show". But after she dropped me off at my grandparent's house, Papa would say, "We ARE going to watch these shows, and you'd better not tell your Mamma!" The hilarious skits and satires made us laugh until we cried. I would ecstatically roll around on the floor with tears of joy. For a moment, I felt free. This was our little secret. A secret that no one else knew, but God.

When I was eight years old, Granny was diagnosed with cancer. Mamma and I moved in with her and Papa. Mamma took care of Granny, administering her medication, feeding her, and bathing her frail, emaciated frame. Granny died in 1980. Her visitation was on her birthday. She would have turned fifty-one.

Papa and my mother never expressed much emotion. I remember asking if it was OK to cry after finding out Granny died. Neither of them cried openly. However, they mourned in their own way. I used to cry myself to sleep until one night Granny visited me, some would say this was her angel at my bedside. She rubbed my head, and assured me that she was alright. From that night forward, I never mourned over her death again.

A couple of years later, Papa and Mamma felt that they needed their own space. No arguments or disagreements, just space. So Mamma and I moved into the upper level of Big Mamma's duplex in North St. Louis City. Even after we moved, Papa would drive across town, about a half-hour from University City, to North St. Louis to tuck me in bed or kiss me goodnight. Yes, I was a preteen, but I was never too old for Papa's love.

When I turned about fourteen, Papa married Robin, who wanted his affections to focus solely upon her and her teen daughter. Fueled by insecurity, Robin began to make open announcements that Papa was not my "real" grandfather—but my "step" grandfather. I didn't know that Papa was Granny's second husband, but Robin seemed to find a special joy in emphasizing that Papa was no longer any kin to me and my mother. He had been a part of my family since Mamma was a girl. Robin's announcements never bothered me because I loved Papa. He was the only grandfather that I had ever known.

Papa's wife was determined to have him all to herself. There were many instances when she would hang up the phone on me, say mean things, or roll her eyes at me. I won't pretend that I didn't do the same back to her out of frustration and rebellion. Over the years, Papa wanted less and less to do with me and my mother until our relationship was virtually extinct.

When I became a young adult in my early twenties, Papa secretly began coming to my job, and we would go on lunch dates. By this time, he'd had a couple of minor strokes, heart attacks, and diminished sight. Things were different now. I had moved on. The past had become so distant—so had he and his wife.

During our lunch outings, I wanted the love of the vivacious, intellectual man I once knew. I wanted to fall asleep in his arms again and tell him secrets like I used to. But now, I was cutting his meat into bite sized pieces. I felt like a nurse's assistant caring for a patient. I didn't want to acknowledge it, but we had become strangers. We had nothing in common. We were polite. We laughed and talked. I assisted him with his meals. All that remained was the shell of the man I once knew. Papa didn't only draw away from me; he eventually resigned from the pastorate at his church. Publicly, he announced that it was for health reasons. Privately, he said that he just didn't like the way his wife looked at him while he preached.

It took time to make peace between Robin and me. Eighteen years after her marriage to Papa, Robin wanted to clean the slate between us. She gave me many boxes of old items that belonged to Granny, which I immediately delivered to my mother because they were rightfully hers. Old photo albums, books, bond and insurance certificates and other miscellaneous items were enclosed. When Papa was alive he lied, stating that these items had been lost, stolen, or discarded after the secret sale of his University City home six months prior. Six years after his death, Robin contacted me to reclaim some of these items. We both agreed that life was too short and regarding our relationship, time had been wasted. I harbor no unforgiveness or hatred in my heart for her, but she could never give back my Papa. She could never restore our relationship. She did try to make things right after his death, and I do love her, but a part of my life is gone forever.

It was similar to the story of Joseph in the Bible. After his father died, his brothers were afraid that Joseph would seek revenge upon them:

<u>Genesis 50:15-20</u>

And when Joseph's brethren saw that their father was dead, they said, Joseph will peradventure hate us, and will certainly requite us all the evil which we did unto him. And they sent a messenger unto Joseph, saying, Thy father did command before he died, saying, So shall ye say unto Joseph, Forgive, I pray thee now, the trespass of thy brethren, and their sin; for they did unto thee evil: and now, we pray thee, forgive the trespass of the servants of the God of thy father. And Joseph wept when they spake unto him. And his brethren also went and fell down before his face; and they said, Behold, we be thy servants. And Joseph said unto them, **Fear not: for am I in the place of God? But as for you, ye thought evil against me; but God meant it unto good,** to bring to pass, as it is this day, to save much people alive.

My step-grandmother thought (and wrought) evil against me, but God meant it all for my good. Today, I am in a position to minister deliverance to thousands, and will continue to do so until I die. Joseph told his brothers to "fear not, for [he was] in the place of God." Where is the place of God? This is a place you come to where hatred and bitterness eventually turn into pity. And pity turns into love. Why? Because God is love. The place of God is the place of love!

I John 4:7,8

Beloved, let us love one another: for love is of God; and every one that loveth is born of God, and knoweth God. He that loveth not knoweth not God; for **God is love**.

You come to realize that people make decisions based upon their mental, emotional, and spiritual capacity at the time. It is my understanding that Papa was probably Robin's fourth husband. And Robin, as a result of her own insecurities, treated me and Mamma poorly. One time, when Papa had a multiple bypass surgery, Robin had his name blocked out of the hospital information system so that no one could visit him. After walking the halls of the hospital cardiac floor, I located Papa's room. Upon entry, and only saying "Hello," Robin announced that "Visitors were not allowed!" She clarified that I was NOT his granddaughter, but his "step-granddaughter"; and was therefore classified as a visitor. Furthermore, she threatened to call security if I didn't leave. Another time when Papa was in the hospital, I brought tulips. The next day, the tulips had no petals. And yet once more, Papa asked me to make some sugar-free chocolate roses. I brought a bouquet of assorted colors and flavors. By the next day, they'd all "mysteriously" disappeared. Robin frequently made the open declaration that whenever Papa died, she would never tell me and Mamma—and she didn't! Someone else did! Moreover, she didn't even want to acknowledge us on Papa's obituary as part of his family.

But now, I am in the place of God. I forgave her, and apologized many years ago—even though I felt that I had done nothing wrong toward her (at least within the past 15 years). Being in the place of God removes the false pride from your heart and you find yourself wanting to help—rather than hurt—those who hurt you. The adage, "Hurting people, hurt people" holds true—even for me. Robin was hurt, so she hurt others. When she married Papa, she thought that she was apprehending the handsome, eligible bachelor sought after by a vast number of middle-aged bachelorettes, but she ended up with a sickly, secretive, stubborn old patient who ultimately lost his mind and died. Her mother ended up getting sick, moving into their house and dying. Her daughter divorced. And Robin has had around nine surgeries herself. I used to be the one who felt lonely and hurt after being alienated from Papa, but now the tides have turned. Now, the Lord has blessed me with a good husband in Pastor Trice, and new friends. The promises that Papa broke, Pastor Trice has made good on—and now, my step-grandmother is the one who is old and alone.

Isaiah 50:8,9

…who is mine adversary? let him come near to me. Behold, the Lord GOD will help me; who is he that shall condemn me? Lo, **they all shall wax old as a garment; the moth shall eat them up.**

I don't dare gloat in her loss, because I have certainly had my share. But I wanted to convey to you how to get into the place of God. It comes through letting go— releasing the bitterness, and the persons with whom the bitterness is toward. It comes through a life of obedience and submission to Christ. When you say, "God, I'm so wounded, but I'll still say 'Yes' to what you've called me to." "God, I feel like I can't take another step, but I'll do my best for you." "God, I want to give my all to you, but I feel like there is nothing left for me to give." "God, I'm reaching out to you, and I just need you to reach down and rescue me—even from myself." If you notice, I never used the word "**try**." I never said, "I'll *try* to give you my all," or "I'll *try* to reach out to you." In some languages, "try" does not even exist. With God, you either "will" or you "won't." As you develop a posture of worship before Him, you begin to grow spiritually. After a while, your spirit will be so high, that all of your troubles seem to get smaller and smaller. The place of God is a place of peace. A place of rest. A place of trust. A place of love.

I could have helped Robin after Papa died. But the age old trick of the devil is "divide and conquer." Our family was already divided, and as a result, conquered. But the

devil can only do what we allow him to. This time, in my generation, the buck stops here!

I have nothing but love for those who abused me, misused me, or oppressed me in any kind of way. I am in the place of God. I am free.

2 Corinthians 3:17

Now the Lord is that Spirit: and where the Spirit of the Lord is, there is liberty.

GRANDPA ERNEST

I'd only met Mamma's father, Ernest, once. Some five decades ago, he and Granny had an intense argument in which he pushed her to the ground, walked out of the door, and never returned. Mamma was a little girl when this happened. I did have an opportunity to meet him, but by this time, Mamma hadn't seen him in twenty-seven years. His mother had just passed, and his sister, Aunt Josie, arranged for me and Mamma to meet Grandpa Ernest. He didn't say much. He was in his seventies, worn, tired, and sickly. His eyes and cheeks were sunken in. We mostly stared at each other. Time had escaped, but by his choosing.

Excluding the day that I met him, we conversed about three or four times over the phone. The last time we talked, I was in the process of planning my wedding. Grandpa Ernest knew that he was dying. He said, "I won't be able to make it to your wedding, but I will leave a little something behind to help out with the expenses." Prior to his death, he signed his possessions over to my mother. He did leave money in a bank account which paid for my wedding cake, flowers, and other incidentals.

Mamma went with my stepfather to finalize Grandpa's estate in Indiana, but she forbad me to accompany her. While there, she met Ernest's brother and sister-in-law. Why wasn't I allowed to meet my own relatives? To this day, I have never met them, and don't know anything about them.

When Mamma came back to St. Louis, she brought a taupe-colored metal workbox that belonged to Grandpa. We sat at the kitchen table and went through the many pictures of his friends and perhaps family. He had another life—probably, other children. Interestingly, we found the obituary section of an old newspaper. The woman bore a striking resemblance to Granny, his first wife. However, she and their newborn baby died during childbirth. After Grandpa walked out on Granny, he tried to replace her with someone who looked like her— and God judged him.

GENERATIONAL CURSES

A generational curse is an evil or misfortune that attaches itself to your family bloodline, and stems from the generational roots of sin. It affects the way we live our lives today, and also affects future generations. For example, if your father was an alcoholic, chances are, his father was, and his father, and so on. One woman told me that mental illness ran in her family. For two generations, the men in her family had become engineers and great leaders in society, but now several of them have gone completely insane. As she researched her family history, she learned that her grandmother used to practice voodoo and witchcraft; and ever since, this curse of mental illness has infiltrated her family's lineage.

Generational curses don't always manifest immediately. In my family, divorce was our generational curse. My mother was married twice, so was her mother, and her mother's mother. In addition, my great-great-grandmother died during childbirth. Generational curses can make us more susceptible to negative patterns in our lives. In **Psalm 51**, King David said that he was shapen in iniquity. His lustful nature was genetically encoded in his DNA.

Psalm 51:5

Behold, I was shapen in iniquity; and in sin did my mother conceive me.

David looked different from his big, strong, super-masculine brothers because he had a different mother. He was a smaller-framed, ruddy (red-head, or of a reddish complexion) shepherd-boy who later became King of Israel. The implied truth of Psalm 51 reveals that David's father, Jesse, was a whoremonger. After David was anointed King, he saw Bathsheba bathing on the rooftop and lusted after her. Yes! She was fine, naked, and married to another man, but the conception of lust had already embedded itself within the lining of David's heart.

James 1:15

Then when lust hath conceived, it bringeth forth sin: and sin, when it is finished, bringeth forth death.

He slept with her. She got pregnant. David had her husband killed to hide his trespass. Then, their baby died. This curse progressed with each generation. By the end of his son's reign as king, Solomon had more women than he could handle with 700 wives and princesses, and 300 concubines. (**I Kings 11:3**)

How do you know if you're dealing with a generational curse? You may begin to develop an inward craving or appetite for something and not be able to identify its source. Or, you may begin to see a recurring pattern that repeats itself in your family. For example, some entire generations live on governmental assistance. Some families have histories of incest, frequenting drug rehabilitation institutions—or even jail. Generational curses can pass down from parents, an uncle, aunt, or cousin—or even skip generations.

First, you have to identify the curse that is working within your family. The Bible tells us that God's will is for a man to cleave unto his wife and the two become one flesh. (Genesis 2:24) Once I knew His will for me, I had to pray to God and say out loud, "I rebuke the generational curse of divorce at its root, in Jesus' name, that it may never spring forth again in my life or future generations."

Jude 3:19

Yet Michael the archangel, when contending with the devil… [did] not bring against him a railing accusation, but said, The Lord rebuke thee.

I may never know where the root of divorce first germinated, but I can curse it in Jesus' name. Later this year, Pastor Trice and I will have been married for 10 years. It's not that we never have struggles or disagreements, but we're determined to work through them. At first, Satan used to trick me through an onslaught of temptations, causing me to consider walking away from our marriage, but I had to resist those temptations and rebuke him.

James 4:7

Submit yourselves therefore to God. Resist the devil, and he will flee from you.

After identifying and verbally rebuking your generational curses, you have to know what to be on the lookout for. Satan and all of his little demons are always looking for ways to destroy you. The Bible instructs us to:

I Peter 5:8

Be sober, be vigilant; because your adversary the devil, as a roaring lion, walketh about, seeking whom he may devour:

If alcoholism ran strongly in your family, you should probably avoid occasional social drinking, so as to not give the devil occasion to tempt you into falling into alcoholism. If seeds of pornography are deeply rooted within your family lineage, then perhaps you should get Internet porn filters, and order the "Family or Sports" Tier Cable packages so you're not tempted to watch late-night X-Rated movies. If your family was generationally on welfare, then a functional budgetary plan could work for you, as well as starting an internet or real estate business. This way, you could still get paid while you sleep, go to school, or travel, just as you did on welfare.

If divorce generationally ran in your family like mine, you must quickly diffuse argumentative seasons and temptations in your marriage, and frequently ask the question, "What happened to bring us to this point." Then, resolve the problem. In a marriage, there is no room for foolish pride if you want it to work.

Your incentive for fighting against generational curses isn't so much for yourself—but for your children, and your children's' children. You want them to have a better life.

Psalm 103:17

But the mercy of the LORD is from everlasting to everlasting upon them that fear him, and his righteousness unto children's children.

There is a constant war within ourselves between what we know is right and actually doing it. Breaking generational curses involves, once again, walking in the Holy Spirit:

Galatians 5:17

…Walk in the Spirit, and ye shall not fulfill the lust of the flesh. For the flesh lusteth against the Spirit, and the Spirit against the flesh: and these are contrary the one to the other: so that ye cannot do the things that ye would.

Romans 7:18

For I know that in me (that is, in my flesh) dwelleth no good thing…

There are always open doors of temptation: The temptation to lie. The temptation to walk away from ministry. The temptation to cheat. The temptation to give up on life. The temptation not to pray. The temptation to watch television verses reading or meditating on God's Word. The temptation to stay home, and not go to church. These and many more doors are always open. The decisions that we make concerning whether we walk through these doors affects our destiny. We have to make our spirit stronger, and our fleshly appetites weaker. The Bible says that if we walk in the spirit, then we will not fulfill the lust of the flesh. What is the flesh?

Galatians 5:19-26

Now the works of the flesh are manifest, which are these: **adultery, fornication, uncleanness, lasciviousness, idolatry, witchcraft, hatred, variance, emulations, wrath, strife, seditions, heresies, envyings, murders, drunkenness, revellings**, and such like: of the which I tell you before, as I have also told you in time past, that they which do such things shall not inherit the kingdom of God.

But the **fruit of the Spirit** [of God] is love, joy, peace, longsuffering, gentleness, goodness, faith, meekness, temperance: against such there is no law. And they that are Christ's have crucified the flesh with the affections and lusts. If we live in the Spirit, let us also walk in the Spirit [this is how we overcome the flesh]. Let us not be desirous of vain glory, provoking one another, envying one another.

"Flesh" (in this context) is the culmination of all the scum inherent in our nature that was passed down from Adam as a result of his disobedience. We all have it. It's the generational curse of mankind. Some days the spirit wins. Other days, the flesh wins. That's life. We may not win every single battle, but in the end, we will win the war!

MERCY IN THE MIDST

With my family history of divorce, I was terrified of marriage. I figured, "If the men within my family who are *supposed* to love me don't even love me, then I shouldn't expect much from someone outside of the family." I thought that I would never find true love. My heart began to harden to resist the pain, so that I would never be hurt again. I decided to use men like I had previously been used. After all, my body was simply flesh and my heart had turned into stone. I was young, but felt old. I was alive, but felt dead.

I hated my life. By the age of nineteen, I'd vowed that if my life was still full of pain by the time I was thirty, I would personally end it all myself. I felt like nobody really wanted me. I was poor, fat like Daddy, struggling through life, and couldn't seem to get out of my current situation. Mamma and I had gone from living in a quiet suburb in University City to Lee Avenue in North St. Louis.

Lee was a former mixed community with residential and commercial properties. During the early to mid 1900's, African Americans were forced to live within certain geographic boundaries due to racial residential ordinances, and real-estate covenants forbidding the sale of houses to non-Caucasian persons. African Americans were only allowed to cross these geographic boundaries during the day to go work for their white bosses, but by dusk they'd better be back in the "hood."

As the laws changed, neighborhoods became integrated. In the old 1960's stretch of Lee Avenue, you could find rows of duplexes, multiplexes, and small bungalows filled with working-class people. It was clean. There were restaurants, dry cleaners, beauty salons, barber shops, and corner stores. A TV repair shop, and Smitty's Shoe Repair & Snack Shop, where you could get a beef, tripe or Polish sandwich through the window. On the neighboring streets, you could see lounges and taverns, liquor stores, small churches, and a corner Velvet Freeze. Everyone knew everyone. Even the neighborhood winos had a little integrity. They would preach to you as they carried your groceries, moved furniture, or even cut your grass.

By the time I moved to Lee Avenue in the early eighties, its glory days were gone. Racial residential boundaries had long since been a thing of the past. With the migration of drugs—T's and Blues (know as Talwin & Pyribenzamine), heroine, and later crack cocaine—came subsequent drug-related wars, prostitution, poverty, and violence. This resulted in urban flight for those who were able leave. The banks began redlining many residents of North St. Louis City as property values plummeted, so there was little money to upgrade their properties to sell. Many were stuck living in the neighborhood.

Most businesses fled. The gas stations eventually closed. Also, because many businesses were structured as sole proprietorships, they closed as the owners died. Thus, Lee Avenue, east of Newstead, became an undesirable, crime-ridden neighborhood. Big Mamma, against Granny's wishes, purchased her duplex when Lee was in its glory days, but now the house remains unoccupied and boarded up to this day.

Over the years, some of the multiplexes turned into crack and prostitution houses; and drug dealers walked the streets night and day consummating transactions. The streets were trashed, and the sound of gunshots was not uncommon. Gang members in groups of five or more, namely the Crips, would dress in blue and walk the streets—seeking whom they could devour.

One day, a group of about fifteen to twenty gang members passed by me on the bus stop, and one of them molested me while the others laughed. He grabbed my breasts and there was nothing I could do. I couldn't call the police, because I lived right down the street and these people had no regard for human life. I couldn't fight back, or I would've been killed. Two people had previously been killed on that same bus stop, and I didn't want to become the third victim. Even though I was traumatized, I *still* had to catch the next scheduled bus. I *still* had to go to

51

work or become unemployed. I *still* had to endure unfair treatment at my job, and *still* had to smile and wait on customers.

Many times I scraped my knees on the sidewalks of Lee Avenue to hide behind cars, or lay flat on my front porch to avoid stray bullets. One cold evening, a neighborhood wino slept in the back seat of my mother's car to keep warm. The neighbors asked what we were going to do about it. My mother simply woke him up; he apologized, and never returned. Ambulances, police cars, bloodshed, family feuds, body bags, gang wars, and hearses were all common sights on Lee Avenue. Many nights, the City would not even turn on the streetlights, and I felt as though I were walking through the valley of the shadow of death. Older men sometimes followed me home, asking me to go out with them—one even threatened to kidnap me. I used to walk down the streets of North St. Louis City on my way home from work, hopeless. I eventually stopped scraping my knees, secretly desiring that someone put me out of my misery—hoping that perhaps a stray bullet would find its way through my head, or my heart.

I was always waiting for someone to walk out of my life. I stopped believing that a good man could truly love me for me. After all, I was rejected and abandoned by a gangster, a pastor, an old sick grandpa, and another man I'd never met—Daddy's father. These were the men in my life. These were my male role models. By the time I'd reached twenty-one, I felt like an old woman worn down by the rigors of life. I couldn't bring myself to love anymore. I was emotionally depleted and during this year one of my dearest friends, Errika, was killed in a car accident at the age of nineteen. My life seemed to be on a downward spiral, yet I was in the midst of God's mercy.

I was dating Kevin. I met him at his job where he was managing a very popular retail store. He was temperamental. We had some good times, but things changed suddenly. It was Christmas time. We went by his house. As we walked in, his mom told him that she'd wrapped the two gifts he had been planning to give his little nieces. Immediately, he grabbed the two gifts, ripped the paper off of them, and ran into the basement in a babbling rage.

His mom followed him, trying to reason with him. She told him that the devil was in him. Kevin cursed at her, telling her to go back wherever the hell she came from. I also tried to reason with him, but I let him know that I wasn't his mother, and he had better watch how he responded. Even though I wasn't living the righteous life I should've been living, the Holy Spirit spoke to my heart and told me to leave—even if I had to catch a cab. I didn't, because Kevin had eventually calmed down—or so, I thought.

I sat on the carpet in front of the television to see what movies were showing. Suddenly, Kevin jumped on top of me, pinning me to the floor. I wrestled with him, telling him to get off of me, but he wouldn't. His mother was upstairs, but she was weak and elderly; and I didn't want her to see this. If Kevin was bold enough to curse at her, he would have been bold enough to hurt her—either during, or after our altercation. Kevin played recreational football and was a lot bigger and stronger than me. In a split second, I rationalized that it would be easier to let this happen and make it home safely, rather than have him beat me or kill me. He raped me.

We had been together for about six months and I already liked him. But there were things I didn't know about him like his drug addiction. Also, he had been cheating on me, and the night he raped me he knew that he had contracted a sexually transmitted disease from another woman. From that day forward, the very sight and thought of him made me sick to my stomach. It would be over a decade before I told anyone what really happened between me and Kevin that afternoon. The first person I ever told was my husband, Pastor Trice. At the time it happened I felt as though I somehow deserved it, like I had it coming. I felt like no one would ever truly love me. After all, I had not experienced the true love of a man up to this point so I didn't know what it was like.

About a month after the rape, a friend asked me to accompany her to take a pregnancy test. I agreed. As I waited in the lobby, two teens were sitting there. One said, "I came here with my friend to see if she was pregnant, and guess what? I'm the one who's pregnant!" At that moment, I knew how this visit would pan out for me. Yes, I was the one who turned out to be pregnant!

For a while, I tried to hide the pregnancy from Mamma. One day, she came home early from work and discovered a piece of mail with Daddy's name on it. I was still on his insurance until my next birthday. She opened it and saw that I'd had an ultrasound. When I came home from work, she confronted me about it. Mamma told me there was no room in the house for an extra person, and I would have to move. I was twenty-one years old, working full-time (although my salary wasn't enough to comfortably live on my own), and a part-time student at the local community college. On the other hand, my stepfather, who had recently moved in with us, consistently transitioned from unemployment to underemployment, yet no demands or ultimatums were issued to him. He believed that God did not want him to work.

Faced with homelessness and the possibility of being involved with this drug-addicted, rapist for the next eighteen years caused me to conclude that the common denominator of my troubles was this baby I carried. I thought to myself, "If I get rid of this baby, then all of my immediate problems would be over."

I asked a few "friends" what an abortion was like: Did it hurt? Did you have lots of emotional issues afterwards? In the Pentecostal church, they showed movies on how sinful abortion was, and how the women in the film said they heard the voices of their murdered babies crying in the night. But the girls I talked to explained the process and assured me that they never had those issues. After careful consideration, I decided to have one. Kevin took me to the abortion clinic and waited for me. I pretended that things were okay between us, because I needed him to provide the necessary finances for me to receive medical attention. In my heart, I hated him for what he had done. He used me. Now I was using him.

The day of my appointment, as the doctor was prepping me for the procedure I mentioned that I might have a yeast infection. He examined me. "You poor child, you have more than just a yeast infection," he said, "You have venereal warts and it's the worst case that I have ever seen! They have spread farther than I can see!" He lifted his glasses upon his head, wiped tears from his eyes, and then walked out of the room. There was a nurse on either side of me. I call them angels, because they comforted me and rubbed my hands as I lay there crying.

I just knew my life was over. No man would want damaged goods! I thought I should just go somewhere and commit suicide. After all, it was only a matter of time before I died anyway. Why sit here and let this disease eat away at my body? The doctor said that the virus was already full-blown. Mamma told me she wanted me to move out because I was pregnant. I couldn't live with the baby's father. All of the other men in my life didn't want me. I thought, "Nobody wants me, not even God! Now, I don't even want myself!"

Upon leaving the doctor's office, I requested information about this disease. After reading, I learned that venereal warts are clusters of growths that manifest as a result of contracting the human papilloma virus (HPV). There are over 100 strains of HPV, but over 30 of them are contracted as a result of sexual contact; many of which are directly linked to cervical cancer. There is no cure; it is a communicable disease, and places one at higher risk for contracting HIV (the virus that causes AIDS). There were only 3 options available at the time. The warts could either be burned off, frozen off, or there were shots that could help to dissolve them. Regardless of the treatment, the virus would always remain in the body and occasionally reproduce growths. Unfortunately, the shots were my only option at $600 each—and I had less than a year to remain on Daddy's insurance.

Since the virus was in its advanced stages, I decided to tell my mother and stepfather. I didn't know how sick I would eventually become or how much longer I had to live. Everyday, I felt like someone placed a torch inside of my lower abdomen. When I shared with my mother about the disease—for once, she wasn't judgmental or religious. She treated me like a friend. This was what I'd wanted from her for so long—for her to talk *to* me, not *at* me. Unfortunately, this incident had to happen in order for our relationship to grow closer, but God knows. We stood in a circle and prayed. My stepfather declared that if the doctor's diagnosis said I hadn't been healed by my next visit, they just hadn't heard from Heaven yet.

Two weeks later, I went to the doctor's office for a follow-up examination. A nurse practitioner greeted me and said, "You're the one with the bad case?" I agreed, battling shame as she examined me. She began poking me—a lot. With a confused look she said, "I have been practicing medicine for fifteen years and have only seen this happen twice, but you make number three. It doesn't appear as though you have the disease anymore, but don't get too exited. I still need to check for the virus at the microscopic level." She left with the specimen, and came back and said, "Whatever God you serve, you'd better stand up on this table and thank Him, because you don't even have the virus at the microscopic level!"

I didn't immediately thank God because this miracle was hard to believe. But I knew that I didn't have any more symptoms. As I walked out of the examination room, the entire staff emerged from their offices and stared at me as I walked toward the receptionist's desk to pay for the medical services. The receptionist told me to put my money back into my pocket, and have a good day. I was healed prior to the follow-up visit and didn't even realize it. I was as the lepers in the Bible. They were healed as they went:

Luke 17:12-19

And as he entered into a certain village, there met him ten men that were lepers, which stood afar off: and they lifted up their voices, and said, Jesus, Master, have mercy on us.

And when he saw them, he said unto them, Go shew yourselves unto the priests. **And it came to pass, that, as they went, they were cleansed.**

And one of them, when he saw that he was healed, turned back, and with a loud voice glorified God, and fell down on his face at his feet, giving him thanks: and he was a Samaritan.

And Jesus answering said, were there not ten cleansed? but where are the nine? There are not found that returned to give glory to God, save this stranger. **And he said unto him, Arise, go thy way: thy faith hath made thee whole.**

Unlike the other nine lepers, I came back to say, "Thank you." One of my reasons for writing this book is to say, "Thank you Jesus for healing me along the way!" Jesus is not just a storybook hero—become—martyr. He's not just an ordinary prophet. He's not just a "good-man." But the True and Living God. (Jeremiah 10:10) The "I AM." (Exodus 3:14) He is Alpha and Omega, the beginning and the end, the first and the last. (Revelation 1:8) He raised me up. He gave me beauty for ashes. He exchanged my heaviness for joy. (Isaiah 61:3) The nine ungrateful lepers were healed, but the one who gave thanks was made whole—inside and out. Thank you Jesus! I'm alive! Not only have I experienced transformation in my physical body, but I now walk in the newness of life that one can experience through the resurrection power of Jesus Christ. I'm alive! I can feel!

Kevin was waiting in the lobby for me. I told him that God healed me, and hoped that my parents could pray with him also. But he started boiling with anger. He drove close to one hundred miles per hour—like a bat out of hell—or a blazing asteroid crashing toward earth as he took me home. I thought Kevin was trying to kill us both, but God wouldn't allow him to. Once we arrived in front of my house he slammed on his breaks, reached across me, flung the door open and told me to get the "f*** out of his car!" and he "never wanted to see me again!" I didn't pursue an argument. God had just healed me and I didn't want to diminish the magnitude of my miracle. I stepped out of Kevin's car cured—and he drove away, still infected.

From that moment, yet another glimpse of God's mercy was made a reality to me. He loved me enough to heal me, even when I knew the consequences of my actions. It began with the physical healing, and then went deeper. He erased some bad memories until I was able to deal with them again. He gave me peace beyond my understanding. (**Philippians 4:6, 7**) He removed my stony, hard heart, and replaced it with a new one.

Ezekiel 36:26

A new heart also will I give you, and a new spirit will I put within you: and I will take away the stony heart out of your flesh, and I will give you a[n] heart of flesh.

Like the prodigal son's father, the Lord came running toward me, to meet me, kiss me, and forgive me of my trespasses.

Luke 15:20-24

And he [the prodigal son] arose, and came to his father. But when he was yet a great way off, his father saw him, and had compassion, and ran, and fell on his neck, and kissed him. And the son said unto him, Father, I have sinned against heaven, and in thy sight, and am no more worthy to be called thy son. But the father said to his servants, Bring forth the best robe, and put it on him; and put a ring on his hand, and shoes on his feet: And bring hither the fatted calf, and kill it; and let us eat, and be merry: For this my son was dead, and is alive again; he was lost, and is found. And they began to be merry.

God began increasing my expectations by giving me new experiences through platonic friendships. I had a college classmate named David who worked for a local airline. He frequently received tickets through his job. One day, he asked me if I would accompany him to dinner in downtown Chicago. This was a totally different experience for me. I said, "Yes!" but didn't tell anyone. I did *not* want to be talked out of this adventure. We flew into Chicago, ate dinner, went shopping, and flew back to St. Louis that same evening. There was nothing more to the relationship between me and David other than friendship.

In another instance, a co-worker invited me along with his mother to an extravagant event, and we had a wonderful time. Once, another colleague invited me to church with him and we went to dinner afterwards. Through these experiences, the Lord was showing me that there *are* good men in this world. I just hadn't met very many of them. He was also communicating that He would place people in my life who simply wanted to bless me. They didn't want to be my boyfriend or my husband. They didn't want anything from me! They just wanted to bless me. Period! God wanted to show me his favor. He wanted to show me that I am just as good, and just as deserving for happiness as the next person.

And so are you! It's not about your weight, your height, your complexion, or your past, but it's about working with what God gave you. It's about confronting and breaking the chains of your past and telling every demon that taunts you to go straight to hell with gasoline drawers on! I wish I had a couple of Amen's up in here, because I'm ready to preach while I'm writing this book.

God didn't stop there! I received two phone calls of apology from the past. One of them from Kevin. In each phone call, the comment was made that I was one of the nicest people they'd ever known and they were sorry for ever hurting me. It took time to get those apologies, but God let me receive them. Soon, the **23rd Psalm** began to really minister to me. I actually felt like goodness and mercy began to take a few steps behind me. Then, **Psalm 139** overwhelmed me. It talks about how God is always there. He knows just where you are:

> Whither [where] shall I go from thy spirit? or whither shall I flee from thy presence? If I ascend up into heaven, thou art there: if I make my bed in hell, behold, thou art there. If I take the wings of the morning, and dwell in the uttermost parts of the sea; **even there shall thy hand lead me, and thy right hand shall hold me**

....For thou hast possessed my reins: thou hast covered me in my mother's womb. I will praise thee; **for I am fearfully and wonderfully made**: marvelous are thy works; and that my soul knoweth right well.

My substance was not hid from thee, when I was made in secret, and curiously wrought in the lowest parts of the earth...

How precious also are thy thoughts unto me, O God! How great is the sum of them! If I should count them, they are more in number than the sand: when I awake, I am still with thee.

Healing is a process that God takes you through. I haven't always been perfect, and my mistakes (and outright sins) have been far too many to count over the years. But once I decided to recommit my ways unto the Lord, I became a changed person. The following scripture summarized the way that I was feeling about the Lord after He healed me:

Psalms 103:2-5

Bless the Lord, oh my soul, and forget not all his benefits: Who forgiveth all thine iniquities; who healeth all thy diseases; Who redeemeth thy life from destruction; Who crowneth thee with lovingkindness and **tender mercies**; Who satisfieth thy mouth with good things; so that thy youth is renewed like the eagle's.

This, my friend, is mercy! This is true love! It blew my mind! It humbled me! God's mercy and love healed me physically and emotionally from all the times that I compromised myself, and all the times I felt so alone. From the years that my fathers were absent, and from so many other insecurities.

Forgiveness is a big part of this transformation. Jesus said that if you don't forgive [others], neither will your Father, which is in Heaven, forgive you. (**Mark 11:26**). We can't just stop there. We must ask forgiveness from those whom we hurt. We are not always the victim—sometimes we are the perpetrator.

<u>Matthew 6:12</u>

And forgive us our debts, as we forgive our debtors.

It's time for letting go. Let go of the past. You can't get it back. The only reason why the past is here is because you brought it here. Re-focus upon the Lord. Remember your first love. The Lord says this in **Revelations 2:2-4**:

I know thy works, and thy labor, and thy patience, and how thou canst not bear them which are evil: and thou hast tried them which say they are apostles, and are not, and hast found them liars: And hast borne, and hast patience, and for my name's sake hast labored, and hast not fainted. Nevertheless I have somewhat against thee, because **thou hast left thy first love.**

Have you left your first love? Jesus is your first love, because He first loved you. You don't even know what love is—not true love—until you experience the love of Jesus Christ. Also, as you turn your heart to God in repentance and brokenness, He will begin to restore EVERY area of your life.

But how do you break free? How do you get started? In many cases, every emotional hurt that you've experienced has added a stone, to build a wall around your heart. Ever since you were a child, you've built a substantially thick wall—a wall of protection so that no one could hurt you again. This wall is called a stronghold. In ancient times when kings built castles, they also built a stronghold around the castle and even the city—to protect it from enemies. The irony of a stronghold is that the same wall intended to ward off the enemy—is the wall that keeps you trapped inside. One of the age-old war strategies is for the enemy to surround the stronghold, and starve out the inhabitants!

Have you built such a thick stronghold, that you are secretly starving for love, but are too afraid to let anyone else in? Your problem is that you won't even let God in! He wants to heal you, but you're trapped—and won't open up! What is the point in walking outside of your house, when you can't even walk outside of your mind? What is the point in putting on the whole armor of God, when you're trapped and there's no one left to fight? The devil probably has not bothered you in a long time—because he has you exactly where he wants you—TRAPPED! You're spiritually stagnant. The past keeps pulling you back into the time-warped black hole of painful experiences, propelling you into the abyss of despair. Your heart has been hurt by everyone else, so why not give God a try? He won't hurt you. His power is like dynamite. It will destroy every stronghold that you've built around your heart and mind. He wants to breathe life into your situation. He wants you to breathe again. But you have to become vulnerable, and lose control. It's easier to control at least some small portion of your life, but let the Lord become the commandeer, and steer the ship of your soul. He won't lead you to the wrong destination.

Proverbs 3:5, 6

Trust in the LORD with all thine heart; and lean not unto thine own understanding. In all thy ways acknowledge him, and he shall direct thy paths.

REVEALING AND HEALING

Upon writing the original draft of this book, I was apprehensive of possibly receiving backlash from the religious arena, the anti-abortionists, and the self-righteous "Scribes and Pharisees," but other people's acceptance of me is no longer a priority. There are issues that plague our society, which cannot be ignored. African-American women (according to the Centers for Disease Control and Prevention) are the fastest growing population of reported HIV/AIDS related cases (growing at the rate of 66%). Many of these women have children, work, school, relationships, and may be underinsured or uninsured. As a result, they don't get regular annual checkups. By the time diseases are usually detected in these women, the process is too far gone.

So many young people are dying. The elderly are even becoming an increasing population of sexually transmitted diseases and crime (with the downturn of the United States economy, and loss of pensions). Should someone else die, or be lost, because I wouldn't open my mouth, and speak of the goodness of Jesus, and how He healed my life?

Everyone openly talks about cancer, diabetes, tumors, and congenital diseases, but in the U.S., the conversation of sexually transmitted diseases remains "hush-hush" and taboo—especially in the church. It means that your (or your partner's) sins have just been exposed. It means that sexuality can be exploited on television and in the movies, but its negative consequences are not being effectively communicated to this young impressionable generation. When you have a sexually transmitted disease, people treat you as a leper, while failing to acknowledge that it is God who keeps us all from harm. The truth of the matter is:

Romans 3:23

...all have sinned, and come short of the glory of God;

I John 1:10

If we say that we have not sinned, we make Him [God] a liar, and His word is not in us.

I John 4:20

If a man says[s], I love God, and hateth his brother, he is a liar: for he that loveth not his brother whom he hath seen, how can he love God whom he hath not seen?

Galatians 6:1

[We should] "...restore such a[n] one in the spirit of meekness; considering thyself, lest thou also be tempted."

This is the reason for the silence in the church. I wish I had a dollar for each time I heard someone testify, "You don't know, like I know, what the Lord has done for me." My question has always been, "What did He do for you? Help a sister out!" Healing takes place, in part, through the transparency of others. But these days, people are afraid of becoming transparent. Why?

II Corinthians 3:2

Ye are our epistle written in our hearts, known and read of all men:

Who can read the epistle [letter, commentary] of your life if the pages are blotted out? How will the church (Christians) become edified if we are too ashamed to convey the reality of Christ?

Romans 1:16

For I am not ashamed of the gospel of Christ: for it is the power of God unto salvation to every one that believeth;

If we hide the very things that Christ has done for us, then He remains a fairy tale to others. Isn't the church supposed to be a place where people of all persuasions can come to be delivered, and set free? People are afraid of being unrighteously misjudged. They're afraid of the witch hunts—not just by society, but by their own Christian brothers and sisters. When will we look in the mirror, and see that the fingers we point, are pointing back at us?

God heals us in so many different ways, but in His infinite wisdom He makes the determination. In some instances, He will divinely work a miracle and all symptoms and root causes disappear with no scientific explanation. In other instances, a doctor may discover a cure. In the Bible, Luke was the Beloved Physician. He wrote the books of Luke and Acts and was one of Paul's companions. God doesn't have anything against righteous medical practices.

Sometimes, the Holy Spirit heals us by giving specific instructions: "Stop eating pork and you'll stop having headaches and high blood pressure" or, "Get more rest, and you won't be so exhausted." I'd even heard one testimony where a woman had excruciating pain in her legs to the point that she could barely stand on her feet. Through a conversation with her sister, she realized that leg pain was a side effect of the birth control pills she was taking. Once she stopped taking the pills, the pain disappeared.

Finally, the part that we don't typically like to discuss— sometimes God doesn't heal you at all. In the Bible, Paul had a disease where puss ran out of his eyes. He prayed to God three times to have it removed—but God said:

2 Corinthians 12:9

…My grace is sufficient for thee: for my strength is made perfect in weakness…

How could there be grace in this situation? God gave Paul a companion, Luke the physician, to provide comfort to his ailments. This was the grace. Paul had a number of 'above average' experiences with the Lord. He was caught up to the third heaven, and God worked "special" miracles through Paul. The word "special" gives the connotation that these were out-of-the-ordinary experiences.

Acts 19:11

And God wrought special miracles by the hands of Paul:

Although it seemed unfair, God had to allow a messenger of Satan to give Paul something that would keep him humble, because there is a price associated with carrying the anointing of the Holy Spirit. Paul later confesses the following:

2 Corinthians 12:7

And lest I should be exalted above measure through the abundance of the revelations, there was given to me a thorn in the flesh, the messenger of Satan to buffet me, lest I should be exalted above measure.

Another example is Jesus Christ. He prayed to the Father three times to take away his bitter cup (His persecution and death). The pain seemed overwhelming, but Jesus later resolved, "Nevertheless, not my will, but Thy will be done." He submitted to the Father and endured the shame of the cross. This was Christ's Passion—His love for mankind.

Contrary to popular opinion, some struggles may never disappear from our lives, but God's grace is sufficient for us. Oh yes! He is able to heal all things, but sometimes He may either choose not to heal, or he may leave a scar as a reminder of his mercy and grace. God's strength is made perfect in our weakness. Have you ever noticed how complementary a perfectly matched couple enhances each other? Even perfectly matched friends or business partners? Where one is weak, the other is strong—yet they make a dynamic team.

Ecclesiastes 4:9-12

Two are better than one; because they have a good reward for their labour. For if they fall, the one will lift up his fellow: but woe to him that is alone when he falleth; for he hath not another to help him up. Again, if two lie together, then they have heat: but how can one be warm alone? And if one prevail against him, two shall withstand him; and a threefold cord is not quickly broken.

Every person has a weakness. It may be physical, mental, or spiritual, but God has designed it that way to remind us that we can't make it alone. To reveal just how desperate we really are. To prove that we NEED Him. To give *His* strength the opportunity to shine in our lives. We are powerless without the divine power of the Holy Spirit to lead and guide us into all truth. We have to come to the resolve of Peter who said to Jesus, "Lord, to whom shall we go? Thou hast the words of eternal life." **(John 6:68)** We must come to the realization "that man shall not live by bread alone, but by every word of God." **(Luke 4:4)** We NEED God's word more than life itself!

I, too, sought the Lord, a lot more than three times, to take away my excess weight. I hated my weight. I felt like *weight* was the one thing that never profited me. Fighting a losing battle, I became a member of the track team in high school competing in the high jump and shot putt. I was never a first place winner, but received a number of second and third place ribbons, school letters, and even a trophy. At every track practice session, I had to run many miles, day after day, and never lost one pound. During this time, I weighed two-hundred-fifty pounds. I didn't look like it, but that's what the scale reported.

As the years progressed, so did my weight no matter how hard I tried. For months at a time, dieting and exercising, I always felt defeated—only losing and regaining the same two or three pounds. Some pleasures that many take for granted ceased to be an option for me. Most women get carried across the threshold during their honeymoon. My husband would have tried if I'd asked him to, but seeing that I weighed three-hundred-thirty-five pounds on my wedding day, that was not an option for me. Also, enjoying a horseback or roller coaster ride was out due to weight restrictions. Sometimes even sitting at a booth in a restaurant was out. Then, there was being the last person to squeeze into an elevator and praying that we don't fall down the shaft. Having to ask for seat belt extensions on flights and doing slow-motion-Matrix stunts to squeeze out of public restroom stalls. Facing employment discrimination where employers viewed me as a higher financial risk than the skinny candidate— thinking that perhaps I would have excessive call-in's and medical concerns. Yes, even after meeting all of the qualifications, and being narrowed down to one of two final candidates!

Most guys, in college, never asked the "fat girl" to dance during the slow songs at parties. If they did, it became very clear that the two of you were just friends. Getting teased as a teenager, and even tripped down the stairs. Not being able to shop at the regular stores. Being misjudged where some people, even ministers, would look down upon me as if I were trifling and undisciplined, preaching about how to diet, and stop eating so many sweets, when they had no idea that I had already struggled with this for years and worked-out more than they did.

Yes, I sought the Lord perhaps hundreds of times in my thoughts, my heart, and in my prayers, but His grace is sufficient for me. How is God's grace sufficient? Well, the Holy Spirit had to do some reconstruction on ME. When I was younger, He showed me that EVERYONE has a flaw, something that makes us all less than what we think is perfect. It just so happened that mine was outward.

How did I handle being teased as a teen? Well, after understanding my newfound revelation, whenever someone would mention that I was fat I fought back. I would say, "I can lose fat, but *you* can't lose ugly!" Or, "Why are you questioning my weight? Perhaps it's your question-mark-shaped head that has you so curious! How about we play connect-the-dots on your freckles?" Then, I began to laugh *with* them which made their jokes about me, not-so-funny.

As I began to read the Book of Leviticus, it was talking about the sacrifices of atonement and the responsibility of the priests. It reads...

Leviticus 3:16

And the priest shall burn them upon the altar: it is the food of the offering made by fire for a sweet savour: **all the fat is the LORD'S.**

Yes! I can do my part with diet and exercise, but until His appointed time, **ALL OF MY FAT IS THE LORD'S!** I finally decided that I am NOT going to own other people's issues. I am going to LIVE! I was even denied approval for the bariatric bypass surgery by my insurance company, but when God is ready, the weight will come off.

About four years ago, I went parasailing eight hundred feet above the Pacific Ocean in Hawaii. It was symbolic that nothing (and no one) will ever keep me grounded again. Also, Frederick and I exchanged our sixth-year marriage vows on the beautiful coast of Maui. The native minister, Reverend Kekoa Yapp, performed the ceremony and his cousin, Mahilini, performed their native dance. Frederick and I dressed in native Hawaiian fashion, floral fabrics and sandals, with white and yellow flowers in my hair and around my ankles, the sand through our toes. We exchanged leighs (as is customary in Hawaii). Reverend Yapp prayed in his native tongue. While we could not interpret his words, we felt the warmth of God's presence, and His love.

A Friend Loveth At All Times

After God healed me, I began to faithfully attend my stepfather and mother's church where they were the Pastor and First Lady. I wanted to always be in the company of the ministers. If they went to pray with someone after church, I went with them. Whatever service they did for the Lord, I didn't want to miss seeing any miracles or wondrous works of God after the miracle He performed in my life. I wanted to be wherever His presence was. Of course, most of my "friends" dropped me because I suddenly developed new interests.

One friend suggested that I'd been previously misdiagnosed—that perhaps God didn't really heal me, or nothing was wrong in the first place. But I knew the truth. My friends wondered if I could just talk about something else besides Jesus. I was no longer interested in engaging in the same-ole senseless drama that we used to talk about. I was in love "under new management!" You see, they didn't heal me. Jesus did. They didn't mend my wounded heart. Jesus did! He was my new lover. He is my Faithful and True friend.

<u>Revelation 3:14</u>

These things saith the Amen, the **faithful** and **true** witness, the beginning of the creation of God;

My new lover took care of me. He gave me sweet dreams instead of nightmares, and I didn't need to count sheep. I was happy. Other people's acceptance of me ceased to have importance. The devil continued whispering in my ear, telling me the disease would come back, and I would look stupid for telling people that God healed me. That was fourteen years ago! I have since had more physical examinations than I care to count. And I'm still healed!

God is a healer. He healed me and he can deliver you, too! I began to feel free. Free to be myself. Free to go on dates—just the two of us. I felt comfortable being alone with my own thoughts and thoughts of Him. I felt comfortable being ME—I was learning who the new ME was. I went for walks, outdoor concerts, dinners, and plays and did not have to be with another person for the sake of not being alone. I felt comfortable being the fattest person at a swimming pool, jumping in and feeling good about it. God's love was saturating me and I didn't even know it. I still made a plethora of mistakes in the days, months, and years that followed, but God's love was tugging at my heart all the time. He was restoring my soul. He was making me whole.

I gave my all to the Lord. Whatever was needed or asked of me at church, I did it—from teaching Sunday School, to leading the praise & worship portion of our services, to developing curricula, and picking up donations. That is when I would meet my future husband. Frederick was the associate pastor, known as Elder Trice, and had the same spirit as well. He had served in the church since 1990. He was a very stern, serious-minded person. You name it, Elder Trice and I did it. We were faithful tithers and whenever the church ran into a financial crisis we were there to assist.

While we were just friends, Mamma used to tell Elder Trice to "check-in" on me whenever she went out of town with my stepfather. He would simply call to ask if I needed anything, my answer was usually "No, but thanks for asking."

Our church congregation was small. As a group, we'd all go out to dinner following Sunday services. After a while, some members were not able to keep up with our weekly tradition due to other commitments. One Sunday, Elder Trice and I were the only two members available to go out for dinner. We realized that we actually had more fun with each other, than with everyone else. So, we started scheduling dates to movies, shopping, and other places.

As we began to date, I discovered that I finally felt safe with him like I did when I danced with Papa. I was with a friend who would not intentionally violate my trust. I could tell him anything and he wouldn't poke fun or think I was crazy. I found that he also went on dates with God—just like I did. I would tell him my innermost feelings and he never judged me. He began to challenge my way of thinking and bring me to yet another level of expectations in my life. He became protective of me, and I loved him.

My mother always said that you want to marry your friend, because a friend will love you at all times. (**Proverbs 17:17**) A friend will love you when your breath stinks, or when your hair isn't combed. A friend loves you at your best, and at your worst. If you gain a few pounds, your friend will love you. If you lose a few pounds, your friend will love you. Even after the newness of your marriage wears off, your friend will still be there—loving you.

Four years after I'd recommitted my life to the Lord, Frederick proposed marriage to me, as I still called him "Elder Trice." He'd had his past relationships and I'd had mine, but over time we became the best of friends and he became like a son to my parents. On February 12, 1996, Frederick prepared a nice dinner, showered me with gifts, and composed an instrumental song on tape entitled "Dionna," because I'm cute and special like that. Since Valentine's Day was approaching and we both had to work on the fourteenth I asked, "Frederick, will you be my Valentine?" He jokingly responded, "Sure, why not?"

Frederick proposed to me five days later, and we married on October 12, 1996.

While no family is perfect, I can honestly say that I don't have issues with my in-laws. My mother and father in-law have always treated me like a daughter that was birthed from them. I truly love them, and they have been a blessing to me.

The scripture that was read at our wedding was the very popular I Corinthians 13 (In this passage, the word "charity" means _love_):

1 Corinthians 13

Though I speak with the tongues of men and of angels, and have not charity, I am become as sounding brass, or a tinkling cymbal.

And though I have the gift of prophecy, and understand all mysteries, and all knowledge; and though I have all faith, so that I could remove mountains, and have not charity, I am nothing.

And though I bestow all my goods to feed the poor, and though I give my body to be burned, and have not charity, it profiteth me nothing.

Charity suffereth long, and is kind; charity envieth not; charity vaunteth not itself, is not puffed up,

Doth not behave itself unseemly, seeketh not her own, is not easily provoked, thinketh no evil;

Rejoiceth not in iniquity, but rejoiceth in the truth; Beareth all things, believeth all things, hopeth all things, endureth all things.

Charity never faileth: but whether there be prophecies, they shall fail; whether there be tongues, they shall cease; whether there be knowledge, it shall vanish away. For we know in part, and we prophesy in part. But when that which is perfect is come, then that which is in part shall be done away.

When I was a child, I spake as a child, I understood as a child, I thought as a child: but when I became a man, I put away childish things.

For now we see through a glass, darkly; but then face to face: now I know in part; but then shall I know even as also I am known.

And now abideth faith, hope, charity, these three; but the greatest of these is [love].

The first morning of our honeymoon, we met a young lady by the name of **Miracle**. She said that her parents did not think she would be born, so at her joyous arrival, they felt so blessed that they named her Miracle. The next day, we drove to the Lake of the Ozarks in Missouri, and at the hospitality desk, met **Faith** who had a sister named **Hope.** The following week, we met **Charity** at a local grocery store. God had secretly confirmed to me on February sixteenth that Frederick was going to propose to me, and our hotel room number the first night was two-sixteen.

Since then, we have met Gentle, Blessing, Noble, Grace who has a daughter named Gracious, Joy, Comfort, Prosper, and four years ago our niece, Angel, was born on February seventeenth, the same date on which we were engaged ten years ago. At my job, I'd even met Gabriel, Michael, and Mr. Cross. God is always speaking—but are we always listening?

God gave me and Frederick to each other to continue to love all the hurt away, but I gave him a really hard time when we first got married. He absolutely could not be human, and he'd better not make one mistake. I kept waiting for our marriage to end—secretly strategizing a Plan B. I always maintained access to secret stashes of money in case he left me (like Daddy, Papa, and Grandpa Ernest), and always kept a job. After all, I was trained that way by Big Mamma, the matriarch of the family. At one point, I even told him that he would only be able to get *so* close to me—and no closer. But he loved me through it.

It doesn't matter what you weigh or how you look. It doesn't matter if you feel insignificant or insufficient. It doesn't matter if you have a mental or physical handicap, have one leg or two, one eye or two, one arm or two. It doesn't even matter if you are the total opposite—with the perfect look, the perfect job, perfect pedigree, live in a perfect neighborhood, and attend the "perfect" church. If you delight yourself in the Lord, he will give you the desires of your heart (**Psalm 37:4**).

You may even think that the secrets of your past are too dark to share with your spouse (or future spouse). Well, I have a newsflash for you: they have a few dark secrets which may be ten times darker than yours! But love covers your faults. Love covers your past. Come clean (with the major stuff) and be free.

Proverbs 10:12

Hatred stirreth up strifes: but love covereth all sins.

My marriage gave me a deeper revelation of how husbands should love their wives as Christ loved the church. When we take a look at how Christ was willing to give His life for us and strip himself of His heavenly glory, it overwhelms me. I didn't know what love was. It is unconditional and involves forgiveness.

<u>Ephesians 5:25-29</u>

Husbands, love your wives, even as Christ also loved the church, and gave himself for it; That he might sanctify and cleanse it with the washing of water by the word...So ought men to love their wives as their own bodies. He that loveth his wife loveth himself. For no man ever yet hated his own flesh; but nourisheth and cherisheth it, even as the Lord the church:

I began to realize that everyone has issues in their marriage, and no one person can be *everything* to you. That's God's responsibility. You must allow Him to complete you, and fill all the voids that are in your life. You must become content with Him alone, and then your spouse becomes an added bonus. The popular adage, "Marriage is 50-50, Give and Take," is grossly erroneous. I know what people mean, but Mamma used to say that marriage is "100-100, Give and Give!" You both must give your **all** in order for it to work.

There may come a time when both parties must lay your shortcomings on the table. "Ok, I was tempted—you were tempted." It cancels out. Let's start over. "Ok, I wasn't the best husband. You weren't the best wife." It cancels out. "I made bad decisions. You made bad decisions." There is no room for false pride. Re-introduce yourselves to one another. "I love you, and don't want to live the rest of my life without you!" A few "I'm sorry's" should also be mixed into your heartfelt conversation.

And don't keep reliving the negative past. After all, times change and people can change too.

Yes, I have the sincere love of a nice, good husband, even at my weight of three-thirty-five. With sixty percent of all American marriages ending in divorce, I would say that the sincere love we share is something that only God can give. He is my best friend. This is God's mercy and grace. I didn't say that our marriage was perfect. Some days we want to give each other away for FREE, but during our most difficult times Frederick was right by my side. We've had our struggles, but the Lord is the chord that binds us together.

Ecclesiastes 4:12

And if one prevail[s] against him, two shall withstand him; and **a threefold cord is not quickly broken.**

THE EXODUS

In early 1998, I had a dream that my mother and I were walking down a path. I sensed that something was about to happen. I was carrying a bookcase and there were buildings all around us, of varying sizes and earthen tones. We could not see anything beyond the buildings. Suddenly, each building began to collapse, one at a time. They did not topple over; they fell flat as if destroyed by an implosion. I covered our heads with a bookcase as bricks occasionally whirled in our direction. After all of the buildings were completely flat, the dust settled, and I was able to clearly see everything that was once obstructed by the earthen buildings. My life was about to change again.

After Frederick and I married we still continued giving in both finances and in time at my parents' church. After careful consideration, and much prayer, in December, 2000, we believed that God was leading us to resign our membership. The pastor, Bishop, was a Ph.D. and had an uncanny way of exploring the revelation of the scriptures. He could break down hermeneutics and homiletics that would make even the most seasoned, experienced pastor appear to be a novice. To his credit, he was, and is, a book-genius. He taught us so many principles about the interrelatedness of life and how to discern between problems versus symptoms in any given situation. He created a new breed of disciples, but we were under his curse of pride.

Over the years, Elder Trice and I defended Bishop and the ministry. We were like the mercenary Cherithites in the Bible, cutting down anyone who so much as breathed negative utterances about either. Ten years had past for Elder Trice in the ministry and seven years had past for me. By this time, nothing had grown in the ministry. Nothing had changed. The scant episodes of significant growth were always nullified because of Bishop's pride.

Proverbs 16:18

Pride goeth before destruction, and a[n] haughty spirit before a fall.

Proverbs 6:16,17

These six things doth the LORD hate: yea, seven are an abomination unto him: A proud look, a lying tongue, and hands that shed innocent blood.

He frequently stated that long ago, he thought of himself to be the fourth person of the Trinity—Father, Son, Holy Ghost, and Bishop.

Every time Bishop declared that the Lord revealed a new direction for our church to take, it failed. Don't get me wrong. Everybody makes mistakes, and we don't always hear accurately from God. I am not excluded. But the members began to grow weary of the false promises, and false expectations. We grew weary of failure after failure, after failure, after failure for all those years. There was always plenty of work to do. But never a shred of evidence, or at least a reminder that we were on the right track. He'd previously had a church in the seventies that failed. And here we were, the next generation in the nineties, replaying the same scenario.

We were constantly shifting from project to project. My husband and I were burned out. On Tuesday & Thursday evenings we attended Theology classes; Wednesday was prayer meeting; Friday was Bible Study; then we had Sunday morning and Sunday evening Worship Services. If you were in leadership, you had to be at church no later than 8:00 a.m. on Sunday mornings. We had Learning Center from 9:00 a.m. – 10:30 a.m.; then Worship Service at 11:00 a.m. Worship Service could potentially last until 4:00 p.m. We would have to quickly grab something to eat and hurry back for the 7:00 p.m. Sunday evening service, which could potentially last until 10:00 p.m. or 11:00 p.m.

This was in addition to working, going to school, or simply being a parent for most members. For a short while, there was choir rehearsal on Monday evenings. Not to mention the additional events, the curriculum development for the school which I did, the Wellness Center that Elder Trice was asked to spearhead, the bookstore, and all of the other literacy programs, computer sales, fundraisers, and failed grant proposals. I even spearheaded a Valentine's chocolate candy sale at the local community college to help keep the church from eviction, where I invested all start-up costs, and created all of the chocolate candies and baskets myself (although I did have assistance on a couple of nights). I was able to raise fifteen hundred dollars in gross sales within two weeks, net was eight hundred dollars.

These funds were applied to the church rent, but it was *never* enough. Year in, and year out, Elder Trice and I were asked to give lump sums of money, over and above tithes and offerings, to keep the phone working, buy diapers for someone's baby, keep the church out of eviction, or fund persons who visited the church under false pretenses. I kept asking, "Lord, are we cursed?" Others were in denial, but I knew something was seriously wrong. I prayed for God to show us the error of our ways.

The Holy Spirit took me on a series of spiritual journeys, but this time it was through a series of questions:

> With all of my step-father's education, why is he so poor (after two decades)? Why doesn't he work sufficiently to give my mother *some* of the basic comforts in life—like rent and utilities? Why did their car break down every week? Why, after twenty years, and two churches, does he have only five members—including himself, his wife, me, and my husband?

I understand that churches go through tough times, but we we're talking about a twenty year period of consistent failure. Why does Bishop ask to use my car almost every single day, and never offer to put gas in it? Why does he frequently ask me to borrow a few dollars? Why did he institute a pastor's offering when our small congregation was already giving **FAR** above what was required by the Lord? When I lived with my parents, why did he bring home only <u>one</u> box of Chinese food for dinner? I used to ask why he didn't bring enough for me, since he knew Chinese was both of our favorites. In every instance, he stated that he didn't have enough money, or he didn't know that I wanted any. Why did my mother have to pay someone to cut the lawn? Why was she still wearing the same red coat (every winter) that her ex-boyfriend gave her over ten years ago? Why did Mamma have to beg him over and over again, to take out the trash? What is the profession in which the woman works everyday, and then delivers her earnings to the man?

In my heart, I unknowingly grew a little more resentful and bitter each day. Mamma deserved better. Although she was retired, she worked two additional jobs after having spent all of her retirement money in his church, and keeping them from being homeless. By the time the year 2000 rolled around, I couldn't pretend anymore. I couldn't sit in church one more Father's Day and listen to him preach about the qualities of a good father.

I Timothy 5:8

But if any provide not for his own, and specially for those of his own house, he hath denied the faith, and is worse than an infidel.

After all, this is the same man who never gave me <u>one</u> birthday, Christmas, or "just-because" gift with the exception of a teddy bear, and twenty dollars. I'd even posed the following rhetorical comment to him, "Jesus told the hypocrites that they were evil, and knew how to give good gifts to their children. You are the Bishop, and you have never given me anything!"

Matthew 7:11

If ye then, being evil, know how to give good gifts unto your children, how much more shall your Father which is in heaven give good things to them that ask him?

I'd expressed all of my concerns to Mamma about Bishop, but she would emphasize that he gave what he had—his time. She also expressed that there were things I just didn't understand. After all those years, time was running out! Shouldn't an educated, able-bodied man possess a little more than just "time" after two decades?

Proverbs 13:22

A good man leaveth an inheritance to his children's children: and the wealth of the sinner is laid up for the just.

I couldn't pretend that I loved him anymore, because I observed my mother slowly deteriorating and aging as a result of depression. It cut straight to my heart. She was always exhausted, and always complained of her arm hurting. One day, she even cried about having spent all that she had. Now, she's losing a lot of weight. I didn't know how to handle this. I couldn't bear the thought of being manipulated or used anymore. I had allowed so much pressure to weigh me down, that I developed spastic colon disorder. After much prayer, and finally leaving the church, the Lord healed me from that debilitating disorder and Elder Trice's prophetic ministry gifting began to flourish.

Elder Trice and I finally met with the self-proclaimed Bishop to discuss our resignation. Even *that* conversation was manipulated. My mother refused to attend this meeting. Yes, I was angry and bitter, but nevertheless calm and truthful. He told us to look around the church, see if we had any belongings we wanted to take, and turn in our keys. He told us that we had one week to do so even though we stated that we would stay for two weeks, and pay tithes and offerings through that time. Elder Trice turned in his keys immediately, but internally I felt with all of the contributions my husband and I made to the church over the years, the Bishop really should be turning *his* key over to me! There was no laying on of hands, ever. No prayer. No well wishes. No open door to return to the church. We were now officially the enemies, like all the other members who left. But we stayed till the bitter end.

We were completely cut off as former members who left the church. But this wasn't just the Bishop and First Lady, this was my stepfather and Mamma. To this day, over five years later, there is minimal communication with my mother, and *no* communication with my stepfather. All because we left the church! We have reached out in the effort of reconciliation and reconnection, but they never reached back. I have even written my mother a couple of letters, but she denies having received them—despite one being sent via certified U.S. Mail. Bishop and Mamma see us at occasional funerals and other functions, and give the "protocol" smiles and hugs, so that people don't ask questions. But there is no relationship.

Psalm 27:10

Even when my father and my mother forsook me, the Lord took me up.

After this experience, my love for God never changed, but I wanted nothing else to do with organized religion. Although I had been with our church for seven years, and became a minister's wife, I had been involved with organized religion my entire life. From the whoremongering pastor, to my grandfather, to my stepfather. And now, in a relationship sense, I didn't even have a mother.

I needed a break! I was judged by the self-righteous, super-religious community who had no idea of the hell that I had been through. They looked down upon me, because at that time, I didn't have a church home, but I didn't want one either. I couldn't tell them which sub-district, jurisdiction, or religious denomination in which I had affiliation. I was looked upon as if I was some unsaved, reprobate, rebellious, backslidden person with no purpose. No one knew how to minister to me.

Even some ministers on television would preach about bastard spiritual children, referring to those who rebelliously walk away from their spiritual parents, but what about my situation? Who will take a stand and preach on spiritual abortion? Who will confront the issues of insecure, prideful, manipulative pastors who attempt to abort the destiny of their spiritual sons and daughters? In the natural, I had a father who did not pour into my life the things that a father should. It wasn't my fault. I didn't ask to be born. But it, in no way aborted my destiny. So it is in the spiritual. I do have a spiritual father, but to date he doesn't even care that I exist.

Countless pastors and bishops began to heavily recruit Elder Trice after our exodus. Many would approach us, stating that we needed a spiritual father, and we needed to be connected to their larger ministries. In the natural, you don't get to choose your parents. Neither do you get to choose them spiritually. That connection is made by the divine leading of the Holy Spirit. We asked God why

He would have us to endure such harsh experiences. He said, "To show you how **NOT** to be!" We went through these trials not only to make us stronger, but to be in a position to help so many others who have been hurt by the Church.

The Lord led Elder Trice and I to purchase a number of Bishop T. D. Jakes' series; The Breaking Point, Maximize the Moment, Keepers of the Flame, God's Leading Ladies (for me), and many others, that really helped us and provided confirmation regarding everything we believed God had spoken to us. We'd learned that Bishop Jakes had been through similar experiences. The Bible says that we are not to forsake assembling ourselves together with other believers (Hebrews 10:25), but what do we do when we are forsaken?

It is all about Jesus. Not the pastor, not his wife. Not the building or the congregation. The believers—we are the Church. We come to the local assembly that God leads us to, and bloom where we are planted until He should lead us elsewhere. Frederick and I were like Abraham. God told him to leave his family and would not speak to him for another forty years. We didn't know where to go or what to do. But we took the first step; and our steps have been ordered by God ever since.

Genesis 12:1-3

Now the LORD had said unto Abram, Get thee out of thy country, and from thy kindred,

and from thy father's house, unto a land that I will shew thee: And I will make of thee a great nation, and I will bless thee, and make thy name great; and thou shalt be a blessing: And I will bless them that bless thee, and curse him that curseth thee: and in thee shall all families of the earth be blessed.

As you move by the leading and unction of the Holy Spirit, you must prepare your heart. In many instances, it will be those closest to you that cause you the most grief. They may not understand, but you have to move when the Lord instructs you to. I was thinking, "Is this love? To disown us because we no longer attend the same church? Didn't the past seven years of giving my all mean anything? Didn't the past 10 years of my husband giving his all mean anything? Were they angry because 'we' left or because half of the church rent payments left?"

We gave to our own hurt. Once, Elder Trice received a fifty-six-hundred dollar check that he intended to use as part of a down payment for a house. But he didn't even cash it. He immediately signed it over to the church, and for what? I used to let Bishop and First Lady keep my car for days and sometimes weeks at a time. After all those years of giving, there was never one question or concern about our finances, or if we ever had a need.

One year, a pastor visited the church under false pretenses. He was from Zambia, Africa, and his mission was to raise money in order to spread the gospel. Immediately, there was a check in my spirit about that joker. He could never seem to look anyone in the eye. After discussing my apprehensions with Bishop, he assured me that everything was okay. But I still had a certain level of unrest about this visiting pastor.

Bishop and Elder Trice took the Zambian pastor to get a new suit, shoes, and other miscellaneous items. The women also prepared a nice reception for him at the church. Although Elder Trice and I covered the expenses, Bishop perpetrated like he paid for everything. Once Bishop discovered that the Zambian pastor's motives were not genuine, nothing else was ever said. Needless to say, we were never offered financial assistance to reimburse the debt we incurred on behalf of the ministry.

The estrangement became so intense between us and the Church Leadership that within a week of our exodus, my parents picked up a broken VCR that they were having my father-in-law repair. He wasn't quite finished working on it, but their objective was to "retrieve all of their belongings from the enemy's camp." From that day forward, Mamma would not even ride in my car. She returned her spare set of my car keys back to me. I never asked for them. I didn't want them. She was retired, but occasionally worked part-time where I worked. We would be sitting in the same department, and I would offer her rides home at the end of our shift. But since I'd resigned from the church, Mamma declined most offers. She would call all of her friends and colleagues to see who could come to pick her up. Some drove across town, just to transport her several blocks away. Little did they know that her daughter was right in the next room, offering to drive her home.

One day, Mamma told me that she and Bishop were "one." So, if I gave her birthday, Mother's Day, or any other gifts, I also had to give the same types of gifts to him. While I understand the concept of oneness and respect, that really hurt! My husband and I had already *been* giving him gifts for the past ten years. But she had been my Mamma my whole life! I wanted to shower her with gifts. I wanted to do special things that Bishop never did, because I loved her. She raised me, and I just wanted to honor her—not the infidel (I Timothy 5:8) who wouldn't provide for her.

TRAGEDY STRIKES

The separation from my parents was overwhelming because it occurred during the midst of an especially difficult period for me and Frederick. It was the dream of the buildings falling flat. It began in 1998.

- In 1998, my Daddy, cousin, and friend died.
- In 1999, Papa and Daddy's mother died.
- In 2000, I was diagnosed with diabetes, Daddy's wife died, and Frederick and I resigned from our church.
- Around 2001, Frederick's aunt and uncle died
- In January, 2003, Fred and I suffered a miscarriage.
- Later that year, I signed a new contract for employment, and the company folded. Also, as a result of my unemployment, the contract on our new home fell through.
- In May, 2004, I prematurely delivered our little son, but he died during the labor and delivery process.

Next to losing our babies, losing my job was the worst—because of how it all transpired. I responded to a job lead from the official Missouri Works website to become a program director for a transitional ex-offender program.

After having signed the notarized contract (which would have increased my salary to six figures after factoring in bonuses), I resigned from my then-current job in anticipation of my new position. Upon reporting to my first day of work, the founder, Bishop Larry Henderson, had disappeared just days prior. According to the building owner, Larry's lease check bounced, all of his payroll checks bounced, and his entire staff suddenly became unemployed—with no advanced warning. I'd previously researched the company, but had not researched its founder. After a personal investigation, Fred and I learned that Larry had been charged with fraud—having written bad checks on closed accounts. We developed a file on him, and reported our findings to the FBI. They confirmed that they had already been investigating him, and asked for a copy of our file. I thought I was on a television show like "Candid Camera," or "Punk'd." I was thinking, "OK, all of the secret cameramen can come out of hiding now. This has to be a joke! This cannot really be happening to me!" Once the reality sank in, I became infuriated. Can I be honest? I was pissed off! I felt stuck! There was nowhere for me to move forward, and I didn't want to go back. After resigning from my previous job, a huge weight lifted off of my shoulders, and I just couldn't go back.

Some days, I was mad at Bishop Henderson for what he did. When I lost my four bedroom, three-and-a-half bathroom house in Lake St. Louis, I was mad at Bishop Henderson. When my cushiony bank account eventually ran dry, I was mad at Bishop Henderson. When the State told me I was ineligible for WIC after becoming pregnant, I was mad at Bishop Henderson. When I was denied unemployment benefits, I was mad at Bishop Henderson. When I realized that I was stuck with two car notes and forty percent of my income was gone, I was mad at Bishop Henderson. When the creditors began to call after I'd strived to maintain a good credit report, yes, I was mad at Bishop Larry Henderson!

Forget the FBI; I wanted to find him myself! Forget the police! I know that the Lord said "Vengeance is mine", but if I could just "lay hands" on him and "stir up the gift" of kicking him a few times, I would have felt some satisfaction. Even in the days to follow, I'd hoped that he would've come out of hiding so that I could just go and set it off!

I was angry with my former employer's hiring practices. Most of the time, before a position was even posted, the candidate was already pre-selected and no other potential candidates had a fair shot at promotional opportunities. I was angry that five years, and about twenty-five resumes later, I was never granted one promotional interview. I grew bitter because I felt like I was tackling the wind with no one to fight. I was angry with myself for working so hard, giving my all and never getting the promotions or raises that I felt I deserved. I was mad at myself for giving everyone else my juice, while giving God and my husband my leftover pulp.

I was mad at God. Once again, I was STUCK! I was like, "Life sucks, then you die!" I had earned an MBA; and had been a former manager, business college instructor, and activities coordinator. But now, I was so pathetic that I couldn't even get a job making donuts.

One day, at a Joyce Meyer's women's conference, a woman named Brandy prayed for me and said, "God wants you to stop searching, and watch Him work out your situation." I knew that she was hearing from God, because He revealed to me that she was going to pray for me. A few days later (while watching the Paula White Show), Paula said, "I don't know who I'm talking to, but God wants you to stop searching. He wants you to stand still, and watch His salvation." By the following week, Pastor Claude Alexander was on television preaching, "I know that you've been searching. I know that you've been sending out resumes. But maybe God wants you to know what a stress-free week is like. Maybe, He wants you to know what a stress-free life is like!" I tried to rationalize this overwhelming confirmation, but was totally disobedient. I searched the internet thinking, "There's nothing wrong with an *occasional peek* at the job market."

I still submitted resume after resume. After all, I'd worked since I was fifteen. But from the time of that initial prayer with Brandy, all of my employment attempts had failed:

- I couldn't even make donuts at the local bakery. The supervisor came around the corner yelling, "I don't need you!" because the temp agency sent me later than the contracted time. I wanted to tell him that he could just keep his little seven-dollar-per-hour job! (That I so desperately needed!)

- I applied to become a substitute teacher with the St. Louis Public Schools. After all, I had done it throughout the nineties. On the day of orientation, I arrived at the same location that I'd previously reported to in the late nineties. However, the entire nine-hundred block of Locust was vacant. St. Louis Public Schools had relocated. By the time I made phone contact, the receptionist said that I would arrive too late for orientation and needed to reschedule. Well, I rescheduled, and later that following week, proceeded to take the tuberculin (TB) test as part of the job requirements. Due to the uncertainty of the results, I ended up having to take chest X-rays to confirm whether I did in fact have TB. The results were negative. But I still didn't get the message, **"STOP SEARCHING!"**

- During this transition, I went to the Missouri Career office to get a job. Not only was this event unsuccessful, but as I was driving off, a small beige-colored spider bit me on my finger as I swiped her off of my side-view mirror. Her little bite served as yet another reminder, **"STOP SEARCHING!"**

- Another time, a friend personally recommended me for a job as a leasing agent. After successfully interviewing and passing the pre-hire test with flying colors, and verbally being offered the job pending my reference check—I was never officially hired. My friend overheard the following conversation between her boss and the district manager: "What are you afraid of? Do you think Dionna's going to take *your* job?" Needless to say, I never became a leasing agent, and the thought occurred to me, **"IF I HADN'T BEEN SEARCHING, THIS WOULDN'T HAVE HAPPENED"**

- Over the years, I sent out dozens, perhaps hundreds of resumes into the wind—only to find their resting place in some obsolete file, shredder, or in the trash. I felt like employers were no longer rejecting me, just avoiding me altogether. Every door was closed. I was unemployed and depressed. But the Lord told me to **"STOP SEARCHING!"**

How many brick walls did I need to crash into before I got the message, **"STOP SEARCHING, YOU IDIOT? CAN'T YOU SEE THAT GOD WANTS YOU TO TAKE SOME TIME OFF, SO THAT HE CAN SPEAK LIFE INTO YOUR STUBBORN, DISOBEDIENT**

SPIRIT? HE'S ONLY TRYING TO MAKE YOU A BETTER PERSON!

I was always too busy. Too busy for my husband. Too busy to really hear from God. Everything, and everybody became more important than my relationship with Him. I hated to admit it, but I would have NEVER quit my job without the guarantee of another—even if God told me to. Therefore, I was lured by the Holy Spirit outside of my comfort zone into crisis mode. Unfortunately, this is how God gets our attention. It is at the point of crisis that He asks the old Verizon Wireless question, "Can you hear me now?"

Take it from me, obedience and submission will save you a lot of heartaches and headaches. Just obey God, and get it over with.

Ecclesiastes 12:13

Let us hear the conclusion of the whole matter: Fear God, and keep his commandments: for this is the whole duty of man.

By 2004, it seemed things were changing for the better. My husband and I were pregnant again. I was thinking, "OK, this is my Ephraim and Manasseh! I will forget my past. I will now become fruitful!"

Genesis 41:51, 52

And Joseph called the name of the firstborn Manasseh: For God, said he, hath made me forget all my toil, and all my father's house. And the name of the second called he Ephraim: For God hath caused me to be fruitful in the land of my affliction.

At four-and-a-half months, I had a premature delivery. He was my son! He died during the delivery process. He was almost ten inches long. He looked just like Frederick from head to toe. There I was, STUCK AGAIN! All of the Morphine and Percocet could not take the edge off of the sharp, piercing pain within my soul.

I was holding little Frederick's body in my right arm, and holding big Frederick in my left, as he cried. I was bleeding to death from an infection. The nurses kept throwing blood-soaked towels into the nearby bin. My blood count dropped by half. No one could help me! I was literally dying. There was nothing I could do. I was hurting too bad to cry. God had forsaken me!

It was during this time that I, still having contractions, looked up and saw a crucifix upon the wall. The Holy Spirit, for a moment, brought this overwhelming peace over me. He spoke to my heart and said, "two thousand years ago, Mary had a bad day and now, two thousand years later, you're having one too!" Then He said that my present suffering was for the greater glory to come.

Romans 8:18

For I reckon that the sufferings of this present time are not worthy to be compared with the glory which shall be revealed in us.

Afterwards, the physician, Dr. Emmanuel, took me off to surgery. Emmanuel means "God is with us." I knew within my heart that although I'd felt forsaken, God was still there.

Frederick and I agreed to have our son's body placed in a mass grave with the other infants who suffered the same fate. I thought God was all-loving and compassionate. How could He do this to me? Am I a pawn in some sick, twisted spiritual game of strategy? Well, checkmate! God you win!

The healthcare professionals suggested that I take antidepressant medications to help me cope with what they called "situational depression." I didn't. I knew that once the prescription ran out, the "situation" would still be there. I knew that it wouldn't take away the pain.
Some sent flowers, meals, and cards. But when I came home from the hospital, I had maybe one or two visitors, after that, no one sat with me. Even those whom I considered my closest friends would not come sit for a while. Oddly, one "friend" had the audacity to ask me for a favor while I lay in the hospital bed.

There were no friends, no family, no pets, no house, no second income, no savings, no phone calls, no noise, and no Mamma. There was just me, the four walls, and the Lord. He was always there. Frederick was there, but he was hurting too. The human side of me felt forsaken, and alone. Like Jacob, who wrestled until he received a blessing:

Genesis 32:24-26

And Jacob was left alone; and there wrestled a man [Christ] with him until the breaking of the day. And when he saw that he prevailed not against him, he touched the hollow of his thigh; and the hollow of Jacob's thigh was out of joint, as he wrestled with him. And he said, Let me go, for the day breaketh. **And he [Jacob] said, I will not let thee go, except thou bless me.**

The hollow of one's thigh is considered the strongest bone in the body. Just as Jacob's thigh bone was knocked out of joint, so must our will, our pride, and our own selfish passions become out of joint to receive the deeper blessings of the Lord. Spiritually, tests in life bring us to a point of brokenness. It was through this level of brokenness that the Lord blessed Jacob, and changed his name to Israel (the nation through which Jesus would be born). It was through this level of brokenness, after wrestling with God, that I began to learn more about the deeper things of Christ.

For the first time, I mourned everything! I had always appeared to be strong in the eyes of others; I'd always placed life's disappointments upon my shoulders, and bounced back. But this time, there was no strength left within me. The weight was too heavy. I finally broke down and mourned the deaths of *all* my babies—past and present. I mourned the loss of Mamma, Daddy, and Papa; I mourned my failing health and my halted career; I mourned all of the abandonment, losses, rejection, manipulation and disappointments that I'd suffered throughout my entire life. I finally had to let it all go; I just couldn't carry it any longer. I finally had to cast all my cares upon Christ, for he always cared for me. (1 Peter 5:7)

This walk through the "desert" caused me to get spiritually thirsty, but I didn't realize that my thirsting was for God. I finally identified with King David when he composed the following psalms:

Psalm 42:1-3

"As the hart [deer] panteth after the water brooks, so panteth my soul after thee, O God." My soul thirsteth for God, for the living God: when shall I come and appear before God? My tears have been my meat day and night, while they continually say unto me, Where is thy God?

Psalms 63:1-2

O God, thou art my God; early will I seek thee: my soul thirsteth for thee, my flesh longeth for thee in a dry and thirsty land, where no water is;

I couldn't explain it. I began reaching and searching for God and realized that I was totally ignorant, like Job in the Bible when God asked him the following questions:

Job 38:4-8

"Where wast thou when I laid the foundations of the earth? Declare, if thou hast understanding. Who hath laid the measures thereof, if thou knowest? Or who hath stretched the line upon it? Whereupon are the foundations thereof fastened? Or who laid the corner stone thereof; When the morning stars sang together, and all the sons of God shouted for joy? Or who shut up the sea with doors, when it brake forth, as if it had issued out of the womb?"

God continues questioning Job throughout the following chapters. After losing everything he had, including his children and his health, Job, being lifted in pride, thinks that he knows all about God. So God humbles Job even more by performing an extensive interrogation, but Job could not answer. He later confesses:

Memoirs of Mercy

Job 42:3 b

...therefore have I uttered that I understood not; things too wonderful for me, which I knew not.

How do you transition from the depths of despair, back to the Lord? You have to take things one day at a time. Some days you will be upbeat. The sun will be shining outside. You will be feeling good in your body and spirit. You will be on guard for any spiritual attacks that come your way. Then, on the other hand, there will be days that you wake up, the sky will be overcast with clouds, you may not feel as strong in your body and spirit—you will be off guard, and the enemy will come at you with depression. These are times when we have a tendency to take our eyes off of Christ, and focus upon the situations around us. We begin to sink. Let's take a look at what happened when Peter took his eyes off of Jesus:

Matthew 14:24-33

But the ship was now in the midst of the sea, tossed with waves: for the wind was contrary. And in the fourth watch of the night Jesus went unto them, walking on the sea. And when the disciples saw him walking on the sea. They were troubled, saying, It is a spirit; and they cried out for fear.

115

But straightway Jesus spake unto them, saying, Be of good cheer; it is I; be not afraid. And Peter answered him and said, Lord, if it be thou, bid me come unto thee on the water. And he said, Come. And when Peter was come down out of the ship, he walked on the water, to go to Jesus.

But when he saw the wind boisterous, he was afraid; and beginning to sink, he cried, saying, Lord, save me. And immediately Jesus stretched forth his hand, and caught him, and said unto him, O thou of little faith, wherefore didst thou doubt? And when they were come into the ship, the wind ceased. Then they that were in the ship came and worshipped him, saying, of a truth thou art the Son of God.

During these times of potential depression you have to pull out any scriptures that you can think of, or just pray. Play some worship music. Listen to ministry tapes. The point is, get your mind and your focus back on Jesus so you don't begin to sink into depression. I personally recall any of the Psalms that come to mind. Each scripture is a punch in the devil's face. The following are some of my favorites:

Psalm 23

The LORD is my shepherd; I shall not want. He maketh me to lie down in green pastures: he leadeth me beside the still waters. He restoreth my soul: he leadeth me in the paths of righteousness for his name's sake. Yea, though I walk through the valley of the shadow of death, I will fear no evil: for thou art with me; thy rod and thy staff they comfort me. Thou preparest a table before me in the presence of mine enemies: thou anointest my head with oil; my cup runneth over. Surely goodness and mercy shall follow me all the days of my life: and I will dwell in the house of the LORD for ever.

Psalm 28:7

The LORD is my strength and my shield; my heart trusted in him, and I am helped: therefore my heart greatly rejoiceth; and with my song will I praise him.

Psalm 46:1

God is our refuge and strength, a very present help in trouble.

Psalm 118:17

I shall not die, but live, and declare the works of the LORD.

Psalm 61:1-4

Hear my cry, O God; attend unto my prayer. From the end of the earth will I cry unto thee, when my heart is overwhelmed: lead me to the rock that is higher than I. For thou hast been a shelter for me, and a strong tower from the enemy. I will abide in thy tabernacle for ever: I will trust in the covert of thy wings. Selah.

Once I get the ball rolling with about two or three scriptures, the rest just come out. After a while, I'm feeling a little stronger and the devil has a black eye. Then, I make myself get out of bed or off the couch and open the blinds. Or, leave the house altogether and go for a walk, a drive, or a swim at the YMCA. You may have to get up and clean your house. Do some yard work. Do something! This formula really works for me, and many with whom I've shared this strategy say it has worked for them.

It's time for healing. Time for forgiveness. Time to let go of the past. God is waiting for you. He's waiting to take your hand to lead and hold you. He's ready to take your heart, to mend and love you. But you *must* let Him in. He wants to break down every stronghold that you've built around your heart: walls of insecurity— walls of mistrust. God wants to bring you into a deeper relationship with Him. We wouldn't know God as a healer, if we were never sick. We wouldn't know him as a lawyer, if we never got into trouble. God wants to show you a higher level of things to come in your life and build stronger character within you.

<u>Jeremiah 33:3</u>

Call unto me, and I will answer thee, and shew thee great and mighty things, which thou knowest not.

Moreover, God wants you to learn HIS character. He wants you to be "…confident of this very thing, that he which hath begun a good work in you will perform it until the day of Jesus Christ." (Philipians 1:6)

You may be a student, a minister or an elected official. Life experiences are common to us all. We each have a collection of memoirs to share. But God wants our obedience. If we sincerely love Him, obedience is not a chore.

I wish that I could conclude this book by telling you I've gone from rags to riches—and suddenly everything in my life has turned out to be perfect. I wish I could tell you that all of a sudden, I turned voluptuously thin and all of my weight-related health concerns have disappeared. I even wish I could report that, financially, I am in the black; and that creditors (whom I affectionately call "investors") don't call anymore. BUT I CAN'T! AT LEAST NOT YET! Some days, I get tired. I mean, really, really tired. Some days I wonder, "Lord, how much longer must I endure? How much longer must I wait for your promises to come to fruition?" Some days, I feel like giving up. But I have finally accepted these things as a part of life—as God's customized curriculum just for me. It has tempered me like weatherproof glass. Some things can no longer break me! Not the past. Not those persons closest to me.

Galatians 6:17

From henceforth let no man trouble me: for I bear in my body the marks of the Lord Jesus.

I have accepted that God's grace is sufficient for me. That His strength is made perfect in my weakness. I have accepted that I must become like the woman in the Bible who had a blood disorder for twelve years. She had been to the best doctors, and spent all of her money. Yet, she pressed through the crowds, risking the ridicule of others—even death—to get closer to Jesus. In the Jewish custom, she was considered unclean. I would imagine that after constant infections and heavy blood flow, she didn't necessarily smell so clean—although she was normally a clean woman. I would imagine that her iron-blood-count was low, and she was weak in her body, yet when Jesus passed by, she mustered up what little strength she had and pressed toward Him with all of her might. I would imagine that she was humiliated that life's circumstances depleted her finances and changed her standard of living. I would also imagine that some of her closest friends, who once smiled and kissed her, now frowned upon and shunned her. But nevertheless she said, "If I may but touch his garment, I shall be whole."

Matthew 9:21, 22

Jesus turned around and said, "Daughter, be of good comfort; thy faith hath made thee whole." And the woman was made whole from that hour.

This woman persevered. I'm sure that there were times when she wanted to give up. But God is saying, "Hold on to your faith!" and "Be of good comfort" because your faith in God, and your perseverance in His Word (and His promises) will make you whole.

I have now accepted what is really important—God, my husband, and all those whom the Lord sends into my life. I have learned the seasonality of relationships and experiences—that every person and every experience is not intended to be a permanent fixture in your life. Some are only there for a season. I now understand the fragility and brevity of life—that we should not take certain things or people for granted. They may not be around tomorrow.

Time is the one thing in life that becomes completely consumed. And procrastination is the thief of time. It has made me ask the question, "Have I been robbed? and, for how long?"

Ephesians 5:16

Redeeming the time, because the days are evil.

Once time is burned—we can never regain it (except for a divine miracle). I have learned that we blame so much on the devil—but most times, the real enemy IS ME!

Obedience to God is the most important thing. It is everything! Relinquishing *my* dreams for *God's* dreams—and *my* passions for *God's* passions. Yes! Obedience is easy when everything is going right. But God wants our obedience even when things seem to be going wrong. When you are hurt—will you still say yes to the Lord? When you have been rejected—will you still say yes? When things don't work out (even after several attempts)—will you still say yes? Will you say what Jesus said in the garden of Gethsemane, "Nevertheless, not my will, but thy will be done"?

I have realized that all I really wanted from the Lord (in addition to fulfillment of His promises) is His presence—and His glory. All I ever really wanted was my Father. Not just my natural fathers—but my spiritual Father in Heaven. He's what my heart beats for. He's what my soul longs for. This is true worship. That everything I do is for You God!

He wants you to seek after Him. It's not that God is lost, but He wants you to pursue Him like the Shunamite woman in the Song of Solomon. King Solomon had disguised himself while he pursued this woman. At times, he withdrew his presence. He wanted her to come looking for him. He wanted to know that her love for him was genuine. So he didn't unveil who he truly was, until he was sure that her motives were right—that she unselfishly loved him for who he was. God wants us to love HIM for who HE is—not for what He can do for us. How would you feel if someone approached you **ONLY** when they wanted something from you? They didn't care how you felt or if you had a need. They only wanted *you* for what *you* could give them. Well, our Lord feels the same way when we treat him like a Band-Aid. We're saying, "I only need you to patch up my situation, and once I have recovered, I'll peel you off and discard you." God wants a relationship with you. Through this relationship, He will fill every void in your life.

We must begin to celebrate life NOW! What are you waiting for? Appreciate what you DO have—even if it doesn't seem like much right now. Thank God right now! Praise God right now! Worship God right now! This is your key to survival. This is your answer. This, my friend, is how you can live happily ever after.

Memoirs of Mercy

Memoirs of Mercy

ABOUT THE AUTHOR

Dionna K. Trice is a native of St. Louis, Missouri. She is the Co-Pastor of One Accord International Worship Center, and the Executive Vice President of Frederick Trice Ministries. She earned an MBA from Fontbonne University in St. Louis, Missouri. As an educator, she has taught both Business Administration and Professional Development.

Since her youth, Co-Pastor Trice has served in various ministries. She has also served as an advocate for the fatherless, seniors, victims of domestic violence, and this forsaken generation. As a Christian, she has witnessed many atrocities and injustices in the Church.

The author's inspiration is derived from personal tragedies and a desire to press beyond the dimensions of unspoken pain. After suffering many disasters, she came to discover a deeper place in Christ. It was here that she unveiled the hidden treasure which had eluded her through the disruptions of life—peace. The in-depth exposure and exhortation in Memoirs of Mercy will empower, inspire, and liberate future generations from the pandemic of silent suffering.

Co-Pastor Trice has issued both a call and a challenge to leaders in the Church, and this negligent generation. No longer can we afford to sit passively and watch as hirelings devour the souls of sheep; we can not lie dormant while wolves quench their thirst in the blood of innocent victims; we can not ignore the silent cries for help from those within the Church and society. **Memoirs of Mercy** is the watchman on the wall, sounding the alarm! No more! No more silence!

Thank you for purchasing
Memoirs of Mercy.
If you would like to purchase
additional copies of this book,
please visit:

www.authorhouse.com

For more information about:
ONE ACCORD INTERNATIONAL
WORSHIP CENTER,
FREDERICK TRICE MINISTRIES, INC.,
or to book speaking engagements
visit us on the web at:

www.TriceMinistries.org

God Bless!

Printed in the United States
61837LVS00001B/84

9 781425 938673